W9-BYH-871

Caught Inside

Also by Daniel Duane

Lighting Out: A Vision of California and the Mountains

Caught Inside

A Surfer's Year on the California Coast

Daniel Duane

NORTH POINT PRESS
FARRAR, STRAUS AND GIROUX
NEW YORK

Printed in the United States of America
Published simultaneously in Canada by HarperCollins*CanadaLtd*
Designed by Jonathan D. Lippincott
First edition, 1996

Library of Congress Cataloging-in-Publication Data
Duane, Daniel King
Caught inside : a surfer's year on the California coast / Daniel Duane.—1st ed.
p. cm.
1. Surfing—California—Santa Cruz—Guidebooks. 2. Santa Cruz (Calif.)—Guidebooks. 3. Duane, Daniel King. 4. Surfers—California—Biography. I. Title.
GV840.S8D83 1996 797.3'2—dc20 95-25704 CIP

Grateful acknowledgment is made for permission to reprint from the following works: "Swells," from *A Coast of Trees* by A. R. Ammons, copyright © 1981 by A. R. Ammons. Reprinted by permission of W. W. Norton & Co., Inc. "Reflective," copyright © 1965 by A. R. Ammons, and "Small Song," copyright © 1969 by A. R. Ammons, from *The Selected Poems, Expanded Edition* by A. R. Ammons. Reprinted by permission of W. W. Norton & Co., Inc. *On Water* by Thomas Farber, copyright © 1994 by Thomas Farber. First published by The Ecco Press in 1994.

North Point Press
A division of Farrar, Straus and Giroux
New York

for Jim Duane, Michael Ortega,
and Graydon Ross

Acknowledgments

I owe thanks first to my mom for her love of language, my dad for his love of story, my sister Kelly for her good humor, and Tom Farber for sharing with me the joy of these conversations. Forrest Robinson was not only a model of forbearance but truly an inspiration, and both my editor, Ethan Nosowsky, and my agent, Anne Dubuisson, were indispensable in making this book happen. Also deserving of my gratitude are Kathleen Flowers and Marie-France Nizet, David Teachout, Joe Ayer, Stephen Ross, Jeff Orenstein, Adam Ballachey, and Danny Weinberg.

Preface

It's awfully dark when you're drowning in cold water, or at least it struck me that way. Claustrophobic from filling lungs, agoraphobic from the void below, I felt as if watching a celestial scattering of my own ashes: awestruck, and lonely. The waves holding me under were big enough, but my impending death had more to do with how little I knew about them. I'd let go of my surfboard, a great flotation device (its leash attached it to my ankle), because holding it was like holding a sail in a windstorm: too much surface area. So I'd been trying to dive under the incoming waves without it—pulling as deep as I could while the foam boomed over—and when I'd surfaced for the third time in a row with more water in my lungs than the last, I was a hundred yards from the beach in a current sweeping an outer sandbar. The carrot-bran muffin and half thermos of dark-roasted Celebes Kalosi awaiting me in the car were small comfort as wave after wave lurched out of deep water, stood up on that bar, sucked inside out, and flipped me like a rag doll down into colder, darker water. The current also swept south; soon I'd have been off open cliff with nowhere to climb ashore. Flipped again, and in the blackness again, I clawed stupidly for the surface long before the wave let go, thrashed around down there in the turbulence, and burned oxygen better used for staying alive. I also kept my eyes slammed shut after that first glimpse of the abyss—who needs it?—and it took so long to climb back up that I finally answered my lungs' demand that something, *anything*, be let in, and opened my mouth. I got foam—part water, part air—and coughed it out of my windpipe as the next wave broke.

Living in Berkeley's wonderfully human gourmet ghetto, selling Gore-Tex jackets and designer long underwear at an outdoor store (make that outdoor *boutique*), I still shared a 3rd flr w/bayview, hdwd flrs studio with my now-largely-estranged girlfriend, Susan (current status: presumed unintimate), in a building also housing eight of my oldest friends—all painfully successful. Perhaps to maintain face in this crowd, I hadn't yet succumbed to the joys of drinking in front of the mindless fuzz of the Weather Channel, tracking Arctic storms across the Gulf of Alaska and listening three times daily to broadcast coastal buoy reports as if they were papal pronouncements from the steps of Saint Peter's—which, in a sense, they are. Only occasionally did I get it together to drive over the San Francisco Bay Bridge, past the tawdry little pastel box-houses of Daly City and Pacifica—sad little burgs on an abused strip of ocean—to these beaches I still knew very little about, and never, ever, did I schedule my workday around the outgoing tide. I hadn't even reached the breaking point with T-shirt folding, tent-stake inventorying, and ski-boot lacing, although I had called a surf report the night before. The scratchy recording at San Francisco's Wise Surfboards was spoken in the kind of California drawl that comes from the back of the throat, lingering on each phrase's final syllable: "Well, boys, it's Victory at Sea out here today. Twenty, twenty-five feet, breaking a half mile offshore, definitely a day for safer harbors." But one hears, of course, what one wants (the word, in case you were wondering, is *hubris*: hu•bris, *n.* excessive pride or self-confidence; arrogance. *syn.* overboldness, imprudence. *ant.* sophrosyne, discretion).

Up at five with cheap thrills in mind—coffee, scone, and that muffin in the car, headlights and radio news on the bridge (housing starts down, man disemboweled in escalator failure, Dow-Jones up), San Francisco just awakening, on the coast by dawn. Delighted not to see a single other car at the beach, I stood pink and naked on the highway shoulder, shaking in the frigid wind—most likely a southerly, though I wouldn't have noticed its direction, still hadn't a clue about air's effect on water. Pulled on my uncle's time-cracked, late-1970s Body Glove wetsuit as commuters shot north and, smugness being a fault of mine, no doubt congratulated myself for having stepped off the workaday Habitrail for a morning. Walking out the dirt road, I felt the sharp gravel under my feet and shivered in the damp night air lingering in the creek bed. A peculiar mist hangs over the coast during long runs of great swell, a fine, almost invisible fog, but I didn't know that then, and wouldn't have noticed the dawn's filling that ethereal field of disembodied sea with soft, hazy red. It was early January, the heart of the rainy season and, in a way, California's true spring. The first radish blossoms were already doing their humble, cheery thing along those farm roads—dainty, purple and white along fallow fields carpeted lush green with oxalis, mustard, and thistle, all a few weeks from bursting into square miles of brightest, waving yellow. But I wouldn't have noticed any of that either.

I probably saw the little cottontail rabbits standing dumb and immobile in the road's runnels, maybe even thought about their propensity for cardiac arrest when being chased and what tidy little meals they seemed born to make, but I'm certain I knew nothing of the smoky-white marsh hawk who hunted that reedy lagoon every day, and who, at that hour of a cold morning, would have been perched on a high-wire pole by the Southern Pacific railroad, waiting for the sun to stir thermal bubbles big enough for his heavy wings. And standing on the vacant strand, facing one of the greatest swells of the decade, I probably saw big, uncrowded surf and thought, understandably, *What a glorious life!* Perhaps the fingers of foam spilling wide across the highest, driest parts of the beach—and scattering the hundreds of waddling gulls—struck me as a little unusual, but I certainly didn't realize that a 6.0 high tide, during such a huge swell, would make several rows of savage shore break impossible to paddle through. Also failed to see that the creek breaching the sandbar between lagoon and sea made a riptide one could safely ride clear out to the break proper, or that waves never broke along that rip, since it flowed in a channel of deep water. Didn't even know waves came in sets, and so didn't wait for the inevitable lull in between, and even if I had recognized how big the outside waves were, I certainly didn't know they were beyond my ability to ride. And that part I never found out, because, like an idiot, I paddled directly off the sand and ended up off my board, getting sucked south at four or five knots and spending too much time deep underwater.

Still coughing from that last hold-down and watching the next wave stand gray and black, veined with white and fringed with silt-brown foam from the flooded creek, I did know I'd drown if I didn't get ashore. The thought came with disturbing detachment: *Huh. I'm going to drown*. Surfboards float, and floating suddenly seemed like a great idea: reel in the leash, climb aboard, turn toward land, and hold on. The wave's lip touched down about ten feet outside, and lances of spray flew past before the wall of white water spun me end over end. I'm not exaggerating *too* much when I say the impact felt like a train's might, minus the splattering effect of metal on flesh. One moment I lay still, the next I flew; it had the inhuman wildness of a surging river or avalanche. My fingers dented the board's cheaply fiberglassed deck as I spun underwater, but the surface did come more quickly, and so did the beach. The third wave swept me right onto the sand, just like that.

Quaking on my hands and knees, I hacked and vomited for a while, red-faced and drooling, then hyperventilated for even longer, and then just sat still, let the adrenaline fade from my blood, and felt the light nausea it always leaves. An hour later, I walked, dripping, back up that quiet road, the hawk perhaps beginning its hunt as sunshine wisped the dew off the arroyo willows. Slouched on the tailgate and tried to strip off my wetsuit—head still cloudy, stomach empty, feeling bewildered and firmly spanked. Washed a little muffin down with the last of that coffee and watched surfer after surfer pull off the highway, scramble up the berm to look at the water, shake his head, and drive off. At the time, I probably thought they were scared. Now I know the conditions just weren't right: swell disorganized, current too strong, wave shape lousy, winds all wrong.

More than a year passed before I saw waves that big again, but by then I'd quit my retail job and moved to the beach. The break with work went more or less like this: Me, at around eleven a.m., in a moment of near-disastrous caffeine-plus-personal-anxiety meltdown, with sweaty feet, greasy hair, and an increasingly antisocial disposition, to assistant manager Sean, a great guy:

"Sean, I'm leaving."

"For lunch?" Sean asked.

"Mm . . . not really."

"Oh."

"Yeah," I said, nodding affirmatively, "so, that's it."

"Hm." Sean looked at me carefully, perhaps even with compassion, then shrugged: "Bye?"

"Bye."

But this book isn't about how I returned to conquer the big

waves—a meaningless project to begin with—it's about an impulse to take what seemed like the last few free years in my youth (before what imprisonment, I haven't the foggiest idea) and see if the life by the water I'd always dreamed of was actually possible. It's also about what followed: looking into the family stories and California myths that got me here, and consummating a torrid love affair with the California coast. Most important, it's about how surfing became for me a way of being in the world, a way of seeing not just the shapes and moods of waves but the very life of this magnificent place.

Caught Inside

Fall

The very longest swell in the ocean, I suspect,
carries the deepest memory . . .

A. R. AMMONS
"Swells"

1

Unless you're a strolling naturalist by nature, or a farmer or commercial fisherman or ranger, you need a medium, a game, a pleasure principle that turns knowing your home into passionate scholarship. City dwellers know nothing about neap tides or the topography of local reefs for the same reason few Americans know a second language: not out of moral or personal weakness but because *it doesn't matter*. I didn't move to the beach to perfect my backside aerial attack (or even just to learn what the hell a backside aerial attack *is*, for that matter); I moved because my need to be in the clear, alive water of my California's Pacific, on a real, honest-to-God surfboard, on a daily basis, had been a source of nagging angst since the first time I'd ridden a wave. And Monterey Bay was all the watery home I could ask for—a big dent in California's coast about seventy miles south of San Francisco Bay. Santa Cruz, an unpretentious college and resort town, crowds the cliffs of its northern lip and ends abruptly at the fields and hills of the open coast. South of Santa Cruz, small towns dot the sheltered bay shore for ten or twelve miles before Salinas Valley farmland stretches clear to the fishing and tourist town of Monterey at the bay's southern lip. As a teaching assistant at the university two days a week, I made enough to rent a room smack in the middle of all that coastline in a two-story shingled house with big gables, green trim, bits of student sculpture strewn among pear and palm trees in the front yard, and a surfboard shed so old it was held together by hand-forged nails. Built as a summer cottage when fields still ran along these cliffs, the house had old-growth redwood interior paneling, making the inside warm and woodsy and pretty off-level here and there. Most of the floors sloped one way or another, none of the doors sat quite right in their jambs, and the whole upstairs swayed gently in high winds. That house could also have used some work: the chimney just a pile of bricks from a recent earthquake, pine floors scuffed bare, black mildew spotting the bathroom ceilings, countless thumbtack holes in the door frames, sluggish drains, no hot water upstairs, and spiders in most of the ceiling corners. But in spite of very low rent, my bedroom had a clear view of the water (the outer bay in one direction, shore break in another) and windows that opened outward like double doors; and with deep reddish-brown walls, floor, ceiling, and even window frames, it felt like a stateroom on an old sailing ship.

I'd lived for the last few years in a town full of familiar faces, near great bookstores, within a few blocks of Thai, Mexican, Tuscan, and Mediterranean restaurants, next door to world-class coffee, and, like I said, in an apartment building also inhabited by eight of my oldest friends. (Nearby ran an interstate commute artery, and in the middle of the night with the city's ambient din quiet the highway made a roaring hiss much like surf.) And those friends mostly nodded with forced enthusiasm when I declared my intention to move to the water; the kind of move everyone will acknowledge *sounds* great, but in a way that lets you know they'd never make such a mistake themselves. But I had no complaints about waking that first Santa Cruz morning on my still-sheetless futon to a fog breeze misting through the curtainless windows, sea lions barking needfully under the municipal pier, and small seas making a soft, light washing sound. Duffel bags of clothes still unpacked, nothing yet hanging on those bedroom walls, licorice herbal tea (I thought it best to quit caffeine at a time of such existential uncertainty) and cereal out on the wooden porch. Green paint all but worn off, floor planks warped and loose, wisteria wrapping up a trellis to the bathroom window—all of a late-summer morning with inland sun just starting to push back the fog. Sat barefoot in the wet grass and read the local paper, even took time out for a front-page story about a PTA meeting. Nodded to an older man—a neighbor I soon got to know better, who had a long blond ponytail and a deeply weathered, handsome face—strolling to the cliff for his daily breath of space. Twenty-seven years old, and I was residing among retirees and the apparently unemployed, without a retail shift or a commute . . . deep breathing an absolute necessity to ward off vertigo. Exchanged good mornings with a white-haired woman weeding energetically across the street. Emma lived alone, I later learned, and quite happily. She walked on the beach daily at dawn, kept a ferociously tidy garden, drove a cherry-pink '65 Mustang, and entertained regular visits from polite grandchildren.

I flipped over the paper and found, on the weather page, a full-color icon of a surfer next to the words, "Swell small, in the 2–3 foot range at the best spots." But where? Those who know, go; those who don't know, don't go: nobody who knows will tell you where to go, precisely so you won't. And *when* to go, on which tide, which wind and swell direction—well, that's entirely up to you to learn. Every surf town has its obvious breaks, visible from the sidewalk, lined with parking lots, and crowded with thirty lifelong locals during even the faintest hint of surf, but a nonexpert outsider's chances of getting a few are tiny. And greener pastures, less crowded and urban, are hard to find: not on any map, not in any guidebook, and never mentioned in mixed company. Permit a comparison with the other sport I know well: Yosemite's rock climber's campground, six a.m., with sky just lightening behind Half Dome; you're loading the packs while your partner drip-brews a little French Roast and a rail-thin, wild-haired guy in the next tent shoves taped water bottles into a giant canvas haul bag—sure sign of great ambitions. You offer him some coffee, but his thermo-mug is already steaming with Peet's 101 Blend; so you get to chatting, discuss weather predictions, swap anxieties and illegal camping spots, maybe even directions to a secret hot spring. Packs packed, coffee drunk, day not getting any younger, you wish each other good luck and go face your respective makers. Now try somewhere on the Pacific Coast Highway: six a.m. again, damp fog dragging through the redwoods, and you're in line at the AM/PM for lousy coffee and shrink-wrapped cinnamon rolls. You notice a couple of nice-looking guys in uniform: surf-brand sweatpants, fur-lined suede Ugg boots (one of the more distinct surfer fashion items, perfect for cold, damp feet after a long session), Hang Ten revival sweatshirts (produced in the current fetishization of all things early 1960s; "Bitchin' Before You Were Born"), and surf-shop bill caps. New to the area and a little unsure, you ask for suggestions. Do they tell you about the reeling reef across that farm? Or the secluded beach with a perfect sandbar? Do they warn you about the dangerously shallow water right at the takeoff or tell you the secret is to backdoor the peak before it heaves?

"Nope," the smaller of the two snarls, apparently pained by talking to you, "no idea."

A little surprised, because you *know* you saw the bastard gouging a Fijian reef wave in last month's *Surfer* magazine, you pleasantly ask where they're heading. They barely look at you; the question has stunned them—such presumption! The same guy, whose mother should've taught him better, grumbles sourly, "North."

Translation: *If I told you, you might go there, and then I'd have to kill you*. Take photo credits as an index: where climbing, skiing, biking, sailing, diving, and white-water magazines identify every place in every photograph, with detailed travel and camping information, surfing magazines do their level best to disguise them: *Delighted you bought the mag, but please, don't ever come here*. A position I've since learned to appreciate, since good breaks are few and surfers are many, but I could still do without the cannibalism.

Anyway, I diligently washed my plate and cup, loaded my uncle's hand-me-down surfboard and dilapidated wetsuit into the pickup, and headed out for a look. Along eucalyptus-shaded lagoons with rowboats tethered to backyard docks, past funky cottages in big, overgrown lots next to neighborhood beaches, and eventually to a strip of road where small homes with big picture windows faced a mile of bright blue cove. Not much falls in fall in a Mediterranean climate, but this latter part of California's summer, when the inland valleys cool enough for the fog banks to stay at sea and allow the coast a few precious weeks of warm weather, still passes as autumn; the fog now a swirling, blurring cloud far beyond the horde of surfers drifting in the sun. There was a delicious crispness to these mornings, the air cold and bright and briny, the sun low and splashing white off the placid sea as small swell lines rolled under the kelp and left no doubt in any witness's mind that the best things in life are free, or at least don't directly cost money, which is admittedly a little different. And so, apparently, felt the hundred or so idlers along the cliff, neighbors chatting over their late morning coffee on little benches, drunks sobering up with a little Thunderbird, joggers keeping their heads toward the water; and all of them, every single one, watching the slip and glide of those boards along the waves.

A crowd of shirtless teenage boys stood where I'd parked, looking lean and relaxed and very, very healthy. Also a few with shaven heads and mean, beaten-up faces, tattoos, headbands, baggy clothes—*jailin'* with whitey's surfer/skater appropriation of the L.A. Chicano gangster style. Enjoying the abiding pleasure of belonging, jostling, and hooting at passing convertibles, a few smoking cigarettes, others making a show of drinking malt liquor for breakfast. Not the virgin green valley I'd had in mind, all the claims pretty well staked and a few too many improvements for my taste, but I grabbed a pint of orange juice anyway, from a little market/home of Chinese freeholders in the Western world. Sat on a guardrail and watched two stoned derelicts on the beach below. With a pump-action BB gun, they had cornered a big wharf rat and were flushing him out for the kill, laughing themselves to pieces. While I pulled on my seal costume, a boy in a yellow-and-black wetsuit got out of the water, picked up his board, and waved an anxious hello to the rat hunters. The one with the rifle—a well-built, shirtless tattooed man with small eyes—stared blankly back and chuckled, then looked at his nodding friend and started pumping.

"What you hunting, guys?" asked the boy timorously, as he walked quickly toward the concrete steps. The sidewalk crowd leaned over to watch.

"Oh," said the marksman, "nothing much, Barn." Then he sighted on the boy's retreating ass and fired. The boy yelped, then laughed, then cried a little, then courageously tried to keep on laughing as if the joke were shared.

With an abstracted stare out to sea, I rubbed coconut-scented wax over the deck of my sun-yellowed, six-foot-one-inch twin-finned surfboard. Then I pulled on that rubber superhero outfit (although mine looked less like the latest from Marvel Comics than like an old Captain Nemo deep-sea suit) and scrambled down the foot-worn, makeshift concrete steps with designated handholds and several posted notices advertising surfboard repair. In the open cove below, waves wrapped well around the bay mouth before peeling across these rock reefs—refined, *edited* versions of the Pacific's rough drafts. During the executive hours of ten a.m. to two p.m., most of the kids went to school and the dawn-patrol surf crowd hustled off to work, leaving only the true delinquents loitering on the cliff and a friendly crowd in the water, chatting and splashing, complaining to each other about the crowds. But none of it malicious, which was nice, since I was rusty. Adults, all of them, I noticed: not retirement age, but grown-ups, watching a few pelicans skim the air cushion inches over glassy-smooth, clear water with waist-high walls lifting out of a mirror. "Surfboards, small craft, and animals," writes Willard Bascom, "can take energy out of the waves to propel themselves by sliding down the forward surface of an advancing wave . . . The trick of surfing, of course, is to get the board moving and the weight properly balanced so that the slope drag can take over the work of propulsion at the moment the wave passes beneath." *Take energy?* But of course. Wave approaching, paddle hard toward its steepest section, turn, and paddle back with it. Feeling the board gliding on its own, hop in one motion from prone to upright, slip down the face, lean to the right, turn up into the wall and laugh out loud at the watery road rising to greet you, step a little forward to speed across the steep spots, drag a finger in the water just to believe it's really happening, and feel the light joy of effortless, combustion-free speed. And then, in the moment of detumescence, flop off the board with—as Bascom would have it—just a little more juice than when you started.

Unless, of course, someone else has jockeyed in front of you and claimed the wave: limited resources, overpopulation, pecking order against you, precisely why honest emigrants took to the Oregon Trail. The tide had dropped enough to lure the hooky-playing teenagers, the boys with grave manhood issues. I'd just ducked out of one's way, and surfaced sneezing water, when I heard a yell aimed at me.

"Hey, kook," said the little blond Apollo, a sharp-nosed and deeply unhappy-looking kid. "Barney . . . you going to get in the way all day?" (*Kook* being a universal surfing term for the unknown, unimpressive other, and suggesting the ridiculous jerking motions of an incompetent surfer; *Surfer* magazine even runs a regular cartoon about a hapless idiot named Wilbur Kookmeyer. *Barney*, meaning roughly the same thing, seems to derive from Fred Flintstone's little buddy, Barney Rubble.) Apollo was outraged, livid, and, worst of all, he was right. In my time away from the water, I'd forgotten the code, the traffic rules; by my out-of-shape sluggishness, I'd ruined his wave. Nevertheless, his fury struck me as almost comical: aside from the fact that I had about fifty pounds on him, how could he know, in this day and age, that I didn't have a Glock in my car? Something so sweet about the confidence in humanity required to shout at a complete stranger, but before I could suggest that to him, he paddled off shaking his head as though I'd just peed on my own shoes and shouldn't be pitied for it.

In a surf town, nothing makes for a finer proving ground than a good break in broad view of a neighborhood. Apollo performed for the cliff-side audience, attacking waves like an off-road motorcyclist attacks the desert, his eyes full of the rage one associates with schoolyard fistfights. Still, he was beautiful to watch, generating great speed on even the slowest of waves, throwing hard turns with precision. A few of the others were equally agile—including one no more than thirteen who was clearly lost in a Peaceful Warrior fantasy, a look of calm intent in his eyes as he drew out each move with long, stylized arm gestures. A dream sport in any life: venting so much steam, giving shape to every waking moment and partial meaning to the future, coming to understand a specific piece of the earth.

And watching Apollo subdue nature, I got the first hint of caffeine withdrawal, of the faint vise-tightening around the temples (terrifying, if you've never been through it). Out of shape and out of sync, with no chance at a wave, I became a breathing, decomposing buoy. Nearby, a boy no more than eight years old, suit bagging around him as he lay on a huge longboard, took a shove into a wave from his dad and made it successfully to his feet. Suddenly, he found himself zipping sideways through the sunshine, and the shock almost overwhelmed him. He screamed in his shrill little voice, "No way! Wow! Oh, man!" with such unbridled joy—so out of the code of taciturn surfer cool—that every man in the water, tough guys included, smiled magnanimously.

"Well, that's that," said a portly guy on a huge board to the proud father. "You can forget about him ever being President."

A square kelp-harvesting boat floated just outside the crowded lineup of surfers, dragging the long stalks of glistening green weed up a conveyer belt that hung off the bow. I could see the reef and its waving grass beneath my board and saw a silvery darter rise up and break the surface sheen. It floated off gulping and choking at the fish trapped in its long throat, and I tried to forget about surfing for the moment, about the game that narrows one's focus: watched the air and water with all the openness of the fool on the hill, tried to let the sky into my brain, and found, much to my surprise, that this Monday morning in September was the very first morning of mystical sign clouds I had personally ever seen. By which I mean that a diving man with broad ribs and thick out-thrust arms plunged out of wispy raw materials into the river that was the horizon, even as overhead three blown eagle feathers spread with delicate perfection in the late summer's pale-blue sky. I'm not kidding. I don't go around seeing eagle feathers in the sky, but there they were, each spine fine and clear with a long quill trailing behind, all below a sun that brushed barely visible rainbows of green and purple through those downy fibers. And *that*, you see, was enough for one day, a cycle of Platonic cloud forms Rorschaching my soul right back at me, because just then a line of liquid green light came my way with nobody on it. I paddled like hell on my nutty old purple-and-orange board—early eighties vintage with a logo that looked like it belonged on a beer can—felt the wave's lift, then had it. Got to my feet, and as I steered that round blob of fiberglass down the face of the wave among several guys paddling, I noticed the most peculiar thing—no look of terror in their eyes! Didn't they realize I could just screw up and kill them? Apparently not, so, gliding along that lovely undulating wall, up to trim then back to the curl, playing the play and flying along in the morning; pure, quiet pleasure. But paddling back out I managed to get in Apollo's way again: he gouged a turn as I crested his wave and we both went down. He came up furious as we drifted together in the foam and current, reached for our boards.

"You know," he said, almost shaking with rage, "this isn't fucking amateur night or something."

I drifted inside, away from the crowd, unsuccessfully paddled for several little leftovers, and watched the tribe of boys chatter, sneak glances. Spray-painted on the sea wall: "Wave segregation begins with you. Get out or bleed." A swastika rambled across the erratic concrete. Charming.

"Say, Bra," I heard a little green-eyed and aggressive towhead squeak to his eighty-pound friend. "You know that second bowl at inside second peak? The one where it sucks out really quick?

I got the raddest floater off it just now." Don't be fooled—this line carries more water knowledge than most of us learn in a lifetime: "second peak" being a shoaling of the reef that produced the lesser of two breaks; "inside," where smaller waves broke closer to shore; "second bowl," a still shallower place where inside second peak waves sucked out and pitched. For a floater, one unweighted as the pitching lip broke, and glided over the back of the falling crest. After a while, I got to chatting with a handsome guy who had short red hair and a pleasant expression and had been getting his share of waves. He turned out to be a skydiving instructor who strapped a board to his feet during jumps: "Air surfing, dude! It's out*rageous*!" From a middle-class family in New Jersey, he said he'd lost touch with his parents, could never quite explain his life to them. (So many of us, after all, living by the same myths!)

Then Apollo paddled past, returning from his fifteenth wave in the time I'd ridden two.

"Hey, grommet," grumbled a potbellied bearded man in an all-black wetsuit, reminding the kid of his age. His face had a heavy-lidded gravitas from years in the sun; he was speaking to Apollo. "We need to talk." The man's yellowed ten-foot board set him apart from the shredders—it might have just marked him an out-of-shape adult, but he had the stature of a legitimate old-timer, soul-surfer. The kid remained defiant but nervous, undisputed best surfer in the water but apparently familiar with the older man and perhaps a hundred pounds lighter. Human awkwardness in water makes surfer fights largely verbal: guys can be six feet apart and completely unable to reach each other, so squabbles often take on the comic futility of shouting matches between potted lemon trees.

"You got some things to learn," said the longboarder, with confident authority. "If you ever want to be truly cool, and actually have people like you, you gotta not be an asshole. As long as you're an asshole, it doesn't matter how good you are. You're still an asshole."

Pith, and it hit the spot. "Fuck you," the kid muttered, paddling off. But the next time he passed me, his lesson in the social contract got the better of him. "Look, dude," he said to me, actually trying to be friendly, "you're over like a deep spot, so waves don't jack here. You're not going to catch anything." It troubled him to condescend, but it was excellent advice and a generous gesture, and he went on, making his first crack at being both a great surfer and a decent guy. "Might as well come out to the peak for a few," he said, and then he snapped. He'd almost done it, almost done a good deed, but as he paddled off, he said over his shoulder, "Least you might get better."

2

Procrastination has its rewards, especially in a good university library. At an oaken table on the third floor of the stacks, with a view of hundred-foot coastal redwoods swaying and dripping in the fog breeze, one quite easily forgets the task at hand and wonders what an on-line catalog might produce under the subject heading "Surfing." Not much, to be honest, but then one might also look a little further afield, leave pressing studies behind and wander down to the travel/exploration section. Browsing through fat, leather-bound tomes with gilt lettering and painfully dense type—tomes checked out about once every decade—I was delighted to discover that Captain James Cook, later killed and perhaps eaten by Hawaiians, sensed in the eighteenth century something of surfing's mystery. At anchor in Tahiti, his crew resting ashore, Cook made an entry in his diary one day and gave wave riding its first inscription in a European tongue. Noticing, as he put it, that Tahitians weren't "strangers to the soothing effects produced by particular sorts of motion"—meaning surfing—"which in some cases seem to allay any perturbation of mind with as much success as music." Two hundred years before *The Endless Summer*, the shot heard round the world not yet fired, and surfing, as an idea in an English mind, already means healing, meditation.

Lying on shaded white sand, Cook watches a Tahitian in a

dugout catch and ride waves: "At first," Cook writes, being admirably honest, "I imagined that he had stolen something from one of the ships, and was pursued." But Kanaka catches another wave, rides it, then heads out for more; and Cook figures it out. "I could not help concluding," he writes, "that this man felt the most supreme pleasure while he was driven on so fast and so smoothly by the sea." So much of his own life spent on the ocean, wife and kids left always so far behind, Captain Cook doesn't need to be told the joy of riding its pulse. And, wonderfully astute, he notices that while the other villagers gape at the European tents and ships, the surfer "did not seem in the least to envy or even take notice." Surfing already gathering the words and thoughts that still cluster around it—absorbed in a clean swell, that eighteenth-century Tahitian has no use for wealth, no yearning for greener grass, no fear of the imperialism at his doorstep.

Running out of in-house research options, I was further amazed by what unsuspecting interlibrary loan officials were willing to do for my delinquency. Like another book delivered from the Northern Regional Library Facility of the University of California, a first edition never once checked out and in no way considered rare: the 1854 *Sandwich Island Notes, by a Haole*, written by the missionary George Washington Bates. Participating in one of the great cultural genocides of his century, no doubt with the best of intentions, Bates writes home of the tropical exotic. He describes surfers in a cliché that endures into the early twentieth century and the writings of Jack London. Bates sees surfers as "borne on the foaming crest of the mighty wave with the speed of the swiftest race-horse toward the shore, where a spectator looks to see them dashed into pieces or maimed for life." In her 1875 *Six Months Among the Palm Groves, Coral Reefs, and Volcanoes of the Sandwich Islands*, intrepid travel writer Isabella L. Bird gives us the same drama: "[surfers] rode in majestically, always just ahead of the breaker, carried shorewards by its mighty impulse at the rate of forty miles an hour . . . on the verge of engulfment by the fierce breaker whose towering white crest was ever above and just behind them." Risk, daring, and conquest—the tropes of Westerner writers scrambling to give an alien sport familiar meaning. Cook, remember, got it right, saw the repetition of soothing motion, the peace of total absorption.

But for Bates, a hundred and forty years before Patrick Swayze plays a bank-robbing surf mystic in *Point Break*, surfing equals heathen hedonism: Bates writes in bewilderment of Waikiki—then just a village—that there were "no busy artisans wielding their implements of labor; no civilized vehicles bearing their loads of commerce." It's the very antitype of a Western city, the only model Bates knows. You can almost feel this man at the ends of his earth, asking himself the classic question about Natural Man: doesn't he ever work? Isabella Bird, in spite of being an accomplished mountaineer (first woman to the top of Colorado's Longs Peak) and restless wanderer, has the same reaction: "no toil, no clang, no hurry. People were all holiday-making (if that can be where there is no work)." But at least Bird sympathizes in word though not in deed (never the type to desert a Captain Bly) "with those who eat the lotus, and remain forever on such enchanted shores." Bates, by contrast, leaves the idyll by the sea and goes for a hike, ends up poking around a ruined temple. "My fancy," he writes, "conjured up some of the high-priests of paganism. It seemed as though I could see one of the deceived and deceiving torturers before me, with his demoniacal visage, his arm bared, his uplifted hand grasping the instrument of death, and the human victim lying on the bloody altar." Bird also gets us started early on surfing as play, as perpetual adolescence: "The love of these watery exploits," she writes, "is not confined to the young. I saw great fat men with their hair streaked with gray, balancing themselves on their narrow surf-boards, and riding the surges shorewards with as much enjoyment as if they were in their first youth." As she watches the sport's aimless cycles in the equatorial light, she wonders, understandably, "Is it always afternoon here . . . ?" And, like Teddy Roosevelt out in Wyoming for the first time, trying to shed some flab among men with the bark on, she spends days on horseback in what she calls local costume—meaning what the resident haoles wore—and yearns to go native: "I am gaining health daily, and almost live in the open air . . . [I] am quite Hawaiianised."

Even curmudgeon Mark Twain takes a stab: at the end of his Wild Western romp in *Roughing It*, after getting hustled into buying a lousy horse, going broke silver prospecting, setting fire to his own Tahoe timber claim, and nearly drinking himself to death (perhaps intentionally) in Gold Rush San Francisco, Twain sails to Hawaii. But unlike his predecessors, Twain the tenderfoot-cum-roughneck actually tries surfing. Just as *Roughing It* offers the far west as tourism, its pursuits as play, it offers surfing as something native we *all* might try. Among "a large company of naked natives," he explains, "I got the board placed right, and at the right moment, too; but missed the connection myself.—The board struck the shore in three quarters of a second, without any cargo, and I struck the bottom in about the same time, with a couple of barrels of water in me." But after a journey across continent and ocean that has been nothing if not a sequence of practical jokes, Twain glories in the indignity; he even sums up the allure that we've heard about ever since, that "none but the natives ever master the art of surf-bathing thoroughly."

When the fog finally burned off, I filed interlibrary loan requests for a few more nineteenth-century travel tales, then walked homeward on a footpath through the redwoods, their reddish-brown bark so thick and soft the forest felt like a moist and padded auditorium of filtered light. On the way up this morning, I'd walked through the same pole-straight sequoias, with high branches the size of small trees, and from a footbridge over a gorge, I'd seen a giant redwood literally *steaming* in the dawn—light catching the mist trailing off that bark like golden smoke. Now, in the heat of the day, dust from the footpath made a similar effect, shafting through scattered sunbeams. Then I walked out onto open hillsides of parched summer grass, rolling waves of dry warmth and dust—hard to get used to for people who haven't grown up out here (Twain didn't care much for them). Nothing in the American typology of place quite corresponds to these low hills without red barns and silos, all with Missouri Compromise surveying—nothing that says *countryside*. (I grew up assuming storybook farm illustrations were of Europe—they didn't look like any America I'd ever seen.) And it is hard to know well a country your culture has little relationship with: no snow, sparse rain, Ohlone and red-tailed hawk country . . . What to call it? One can't go around living in a place called The West all the time, and these dry climates need room, don't effuse enough spontaneous green to fill up empty fields between mall and housing tract with local wildernesses. One minimart and parking lot can overwhelm a whole valley, leave its beaten-down little scraps of grass looking horribly forlorn. But with their unbroken views across the blue bay to Monterey, these hillsides were plenty to let the mind spread without anxiety of loss, to get sucked into the gentle, arid warmth, the plain elegance of that oak tree in the field.

Down at my local beach, the dusk sprayed red under a fleecy, unthreatening cloud, and the wettest sand caught the sun's orange like a stained-glass window. A fierce little dog charged the placid sea, leapt in after a stick, then ran to a woman in a camouflage jacket. An anxious-looking man, also in camouflage, scanned the sand with a metal detector; he stopped suddenly and crouched down. The woman and dog struggled and thrashed over a strand of kelp as restaurants lit up the pier just north. Out in the chromium blue, the single white brushstroke of a lone sailboat leaned in the evening land breeze, and the sea was truly flat, no shore break at all. But later, through my open bedroom windows, it began to wake up. The upstairs of this old redwood house rocked with my housemate and her man, the baying of the sea lions matched them, and, over time, steadily louder waves: first just a gentle washing, then the smallest hollow "whump."

3

If a surf break can be a Walden Pond, a material synecdoche of all one finds mysterious and delightful about the world, then I found mine through a guy who hated it there. Skinny's real name was Warren Cohn, but he'd been called Skinny since the eighth grade, the same year he'd ceased being skinny. We hadn't been much of friends in high school, but we had gone to one Grateful Dead concert together. Our history teacher had had two extra tickets, and picked us both up at eight a.m. for the Grass Valley Fairgrounds show. Strung-out, sunken-eyed Mr. Wells did seventy-five up Route 80 with a Mickey's Malt Liquor between his legs, steered with his elbows while lighting a bowl of home-grown Colombian. I just cowered in the backseat, wondering what my parents would think (this being, of course, the downside of a very 1970s upbringing in Berkeley), and Skinny gobbled a pile of hallucinogenic mushrooms. The pile turned out to be a tad too big, because after the first couple of songs, he left the concert and wandered alone to the highway. Mr. Wells thought Skinny'd been killed or kidnapped, became utterly frantic over how it would all look to the school administration. But it turned out Skinny'd just decided he wanted to go home, hitchhiked the whole way with the world flowing by in trails of green-and-blue light.

A career surfer and general ne'er-do-well with a wide, square-toothed Cheshire cat grin, Skinny kindly flagged me down on a Santa Cruz street a few weeks after I moved to town. He'd made his yearly income of seven grand, he told me, on a summer trail crew in Oregon while the surf was small, killed a couple of months surfing perfect Costa Rica, was back for the winter. Beached his trailer for a hundred a month in a local trailer park and mostly just watched hoops games, ate Cap'n Crunch, and smoked weed. He also listened to his weather radio full-time, stayed on top of the buoy reports, and told me that day in the street that a high pressure off Washington might move into Idaho and give us offshore winds. He offered to do a little dawn-patrolling with me, which had great appeal, given how little of the area I knew and how many two-hour, two-wave misery sessions I'd been having at Pleasure Point. So the next morning, I drove up to get Skinny in the dark before sunup. On a narrow Santa Cruz street of unexceptional bungalows and big redwoods, night sky reddening over Salinas, I pulled into his gravel lot and turned off my headlights. Twenty-nine years old and Skinny closed the trailer door quickly behind him as he stepped out, wouldn't give me a peek inside. *Nobody* saw its inside, he said, not even his schoolteacher girlfriend. He didn't even like her to visit, found it too hard to explain everything. Best to keep it all at her place.

I put my board and wetsuit in the padded back of the jacked-up, snow-tired, mud-splattered, 4WD Toyota pickup which he'd weatherized with surf-company stickers: Biotribe, Unitryb, World Jungle, Hunters and Gatherers. Immediately, I felt the pleasure of having a surf buddy, of being in the cockpit with a guy who knew his way around. We stopped for cakey blueberry muffins and weak coffee, then cruised town and talked about high school and our mutual migration to the coast. Skinny had a quick, roguish sense of humor and remembered that Grateful Dead show mostly for the mouthful of peanut butter he'd eaten to make the mushrooms palatable. We wound along the cliff, past cheerful stucco and stone houses, and Skinny said he didn't like the wind on the water, figured there'd soon be too many guys at these urban breaks anyway. So, north out of town on a highway with parched hills on the right, planted fields on the left, and the fog boiling just offshore. We passed several little clusters of pickups at obvious breaks, and each time Skinny demurred: too many cars, swell direction wrong, wind wrong. Soon, getting antsy, I asked about a turnout with no cars, the one at which I'd made passing acquaintance with the Reaper.

"It's called the Point," Skinny said, zipping right past. "That place sucks."

"But there's nobody out there."

"Burgery, boily—it's a poopy puppy," he said with a grin. "Not for me."

This apparently meant the waves weren't up to standard, so I decided to leave the near-death story for another time. But when we'd driven clear to the northern county line and found nothing, I told Skinny I'd like to just get wet, if he didn't mind. Wasn't set on finding anything perfect, just felt like going surfing. So he decided to give the Point another chance. Near a copse of eucalyptus and some tawdry farm barracks with broken windows, we pulled the boards out and I packed my knapsack with wetsuit, towel, wax, sunscreen, Powerbar, and carrot juice. There were a few other cars in the gravel lot now, including a Japanese pickup, an old El Camino, and a Buick sedan. With the sun just peeking up and light washing color through the darkness, we started out to the place where I ended up spending much of the following year. Ambled along a dirt road lined with hemlock all withered in this black, tarry way it has of looking like an Agent Orange victim, kicked through the weeds and picked up pricklers from the golden-parched grass. The whole place messy and overgrown, a little garbage here and there, but mostly just a glorious little stretch of world nobody'd bothered to name. To the right were rows of brussels sprouts with sprinklers gushing overhead; to the left, a lovely creekway through tule bulrushes to a lagoon protected from the surf by the kind of sandbar that closes off every watershed on this coast. In the brackish shallows stood a snowy egret, dainty and vulnerable with the garish beauty of a fragile movie star in a white feather boa. Willows lined the north-south railway ditch, and a frog croaked in its stagnating algae-covered water. Nothing wrong with train tracks, by the way—a hundred years ago, they might have been harbingers of modernity in the American garden, but now they just seemed the familiar garden path. And little yellow buds that looked like chamomile filled up the center patch of the dirt road (I picked a pocketful for tea, later boiled and strained it only to discover it was a kind of fool's chamomile). Still, great to smell that parched, wheaty California summer right up against the kelpy sea, while off to the south, across Monterey Bay, the mountains behind faux-bohemian Carmel stood half-hidden by the fog.

The combination of lagoon and sandspit, rocky point and submerged reef and trickling creek was, in fact, the perfect coastal unit, an exact microcosm of the whole northern Californian coast—and so, of course, more than enough world for me. To the right, the Point reached out to a natural arch; in the half cove protected by it, four small waves lifted through a kelp bed while in the breaking day stood three other guys, sweatshirt hoods low over their eyes, shaking out their wetsuits—just loitering in God's country as if it was their old backyard. I decided right then, on the spot, that I too wanted to become vaguely bored by this place, to drink so much of its daily beauty I no longer felt that remorse you often get from visiting magnificence, about how you really ought to change your life to include such places and moments, but know perfectly well you won't. Like finding the thing you didn't quite know you were looking for: that cove brushed aside everything else about the sport and left me delighted by a few low, spread-out cypress trees—leaning forever in the wind the way those trees do—and a muddy trail leading down a blackberry-brambled gully to the water.

"Oooh," Skinny said, looking at the small, empty surf, "it's *draining*."

"Hmm?"

"The reef, kooky. It's draining—not. I'm joking and you don't even know I'm joking." We scrambled down the loose path of squashed succulents as the gray Pacific warmed into blue and arcs of spray shot up the cliff. The wetsuits were cold, clammy, wet, and sandy from three days' use, but in spite of the squalor of his trailer, Skinny had this amazing hang-up about making sure his wetsuit didn't contain a single grain of sand or blade of grass. He stood on a sheet of plastic (for clean feet) with his pants off and towel around his waist, shaking and brushing at the neoprene without the slightest haste. When he'd finally gotten his whole program together, we stepped into the water and, immediately, I took a wave on the head and came up with board in hand, scratching at the water and panting, another stupid littoral current pulling me toward a rock. Facing another wave, I swam downward with eyes closed as per usual, then felt a gross sucking as the twisted curve passed over. I surfaced with a nauseating sense of déjà vu, right in front of a barnacled sea stack, with yet another wave rolling in. Dove and pulled, then felt that reverse gravity drawing back up; then it let go, and I drifted out to sea in a quirk in the current.

One of the other guys in the water, a medium-built middle-aged man with a deeply lined but somehow boyish face, caught a remarkable number of waves, I'd noticed. Two hours went by watching him and a friend of his, a lithe, brown-haired man who surfed with remarkable grace and speed. I hooted once as the latter flew past, but Skinny glared: apparently you had to play it cool. Still, hard to believe the life these guys were leading—both apparently in their early forties, about the age of my father's youngest brother, the one who'd given me the board and wetsuit—out in the water midday, midweek, far from the madding crowds. They called out to each other in Spanish ("*¡Coño!*"), French ("*Cette vague-ci, c'est la mienne!*"), and in some Italian I couldn't catch; took obvious pleasure in one another's company. The recalcitrance of surfers in the water combines with the fact that boards and wetsuits all look more or less the same to obscure real-world identity; you learn to read inflection and expression. The smaller, darker one flashed a smile at Skinny and me that was part soft and delirious, part oddly sardonic; but one doesn't have time to talk, so I just drifted around and caught a few waves that were fast but oddly, organically shaped, with big, bubbling upwellings under their steep spots, then slow, open shoulders. Still, great to be gliding along those rolling walls in a clean wilderness with the sun rising over the sea and not a building or road in sight—at least not from below the cliff, but that's what counts, since it's important to be open to reality management and take pleasure in views or angles that fabricate wildness, like driving through your town strictly on streets that confirm your best sense of where you live.

Skinny rode several warbling, shifting mounds of wave and seemed increasingly irritated by the whole scene. Neither of us could quite figure out where to wait—kept being out of position, unable to catch the better waves. He grumbled something about remembering why he usually avoided this place and said somebody ought to fix the reef out here with a little dynamite. Leonard Lueras writes, in *Surfing, the Ultimate Pleasure*, that ancient Hawaiians prayed for surf by swatting the water with *pōhuehue*, beach morning-glory strands; hoping their ripples would be answered by bigger ones, they chanted (and Lueras translates), "Kū mai! Kū mai! Ka nalu nui mai Kahiki mai, (Arise, arise you great surfs from Kahiki,) Alo poʻipū! Ku mai ka pōhuehue, (The powerful curling waves. Arise with the pōhuehue.) Hū! Kai koʻo loa. (Well up, long raging surf.)." Picking the right branch, walking to the flat water, begging for a pulse from the great beyond. Lashing away in reverence and frustration, watching one's own little rills dissipate . . . Sitting on his board, looking west, Skinny wound up and slapped the water hard, spraying drops in a broad arc.

Being hopeful by disposition, I paddled for a rill he'd ignored, but it rolled on under and I crawled back, head low.

"Sweet, huh?" that older guy asked, meaning the sunshine and clean air. Another wave rolled in and he took it.

Skinny went for the next but couldn't quite catch it. When he'd stopped trying, he spun around with bits of spittle on his lips and his face a mask of rage. "Two *fucking* months in Costa Rica," he said, "surfing perfection. I come back, and where do I end up? In this *shit*." He turned back, slapped hard at the water, and screamed to the Pacific, "*Come on, whore!*"

An otter—doglike and dogsized little mustelid—backstroked nearby with awfully anthropomorphic repose. He had a rock on his belly and kept slamming a mussel shell down on it, then gnawing at the crack; though doubtless cold and fraught with danger, the otter's life was quite a recommendation for the neighborhood. Once shivering and tired, I rode an already-broken wave to get back in. When it lifted up over the rock shelf, I leaned back and stumbled onto the reef, my equilibrium still adjusted to a surging liquid. The very low tide had exposed mossy reefs and pools of anemones, and I walked slipping and splashing among slimy boulders hung with limp sea grass. Sat on a shelf of shale and waited for Skinny, got this funny feeling about the whole place, like I didn't see myself surfing anywhere else any time soon. As we changed, Skinny said something about preferring high performance waves, how he found this reef a little mushburgery and lumpy. Most of the guys he surfed with, apparently, outright refused to come here; he'd only agreed because he thought it might be nice for me to get away from town. As he spoke, the day flushed broad and bright across the water, and the sky's open blue shone in little puddles; I didn't tell Skinny, but I really couldn't believe the whole thing, the whole gift of California at the end of the twentieth century, alive and available in a little place by a little highway with no sign.

The two older guys changed quickly and efficiently, each with a plastic bag to stand on and a tidy little backpack full of essentials. They strolled off with just a nod long before Skinny had dried each individual toe enough for us to follow. Walking back the sprinkler-soaked, muddy road between fields, board under one arm, I heard the low chugging rumble of the Southern Pacific rolling down from San Francisco. For some reason, I saw us from above or afar and knew I was alive in a moment I'd dreamed of and wanted to inhabit absolutely; so often one says to oneself, This is it!, and yet feels, with disappointment, no different from before. But surfboards and dirt roads and farms and trains hit some giant, perfect chord for me, made me crazy with desire to be alive enough to somehow *be* the moment itself.

"Dude!" I said. "You hear that?"

"What?"

"Don't you want to see the train?"

"What?"

Hundreds of gulls swirled overhead when I started running. Right before the tracks, my left foot sank in mud to the calf, the sandal vanished, and my sock foot came out and sank again. The other did the same, and I ended up with both feet buried in muck, holding the surfboard in one hand and waving with the other while I grinned like a fool at the engineer. He politely waved back.

The sandals took a little work to locate and excavate—they still don't look the same—and as I strolled along, toes squishing in my sodden socks, I told Skinny how I wished they grew something more appetizing here than brussels sprouts. I'd have gone home with my pockets stuffed.

4

In one old snapshot of my father, there's quite a resemblance—he's a few years younger than I am now, and reading Richard Henry Dana's *Two Years Before the Mast* in his bunk aboard the aircraft carrier *Oriskany*. One of those rare pictures in which parent and child can, for a moment, be the same age; and I do have his nose and eyes, his knit brow while reading. Dad hated the service, still gets a surprising bitterness in his voice when the subject comes up, but it could've been worse: a few years earlier and he would've gone to Korea, a few later, Vietnam. And he did see quite a lot of the world without having to kill anybody, did his tour as an air traffic controller and was discharged in Europe. He came home for law school soon after, and met my mom. But growing up on the beach in a Los Angeles profoundly different from today's—Santa Monica and Hollywood actually separate towns, Orange County actually orange orchards—he had a mother who didn't equivocate. Cheerful New York Irish with a dynamite sense of humor, Grandma Duane nevertheless held firm on one point: "The men in our family join the Navy." His father, Dad no doubt mused, had not. But somehow that was beside the point, or was precisely the point.

Dad and his younger brothers grew up surfing and bodysurfing, but he eventually left the beach for college and that tour at sea.

If anyone's responsible for my obsession with water and the free time to enjoy it, he is: he had always loved coyote stories, tales of man somehow beyond the fold, *out there*. Like the lawyer friend who conducted his federal appellate practice from a cabin in the Sierra Nevada foothills, or the man who took a one-year position as legal adviser to the parliament of the Republic of Pongo Pongo and never came back. We took pleasure in imagining the guy pushing a raft from island to island, chatting with fishermen and trying once every few months to remember his last name. Or the time Dad had been climbing at Joshua Tree for a week, living out of his car in the high desert: hot days, freezing nights. Over at a trailer park for groceries, chatting with the older woman behind the register—she said her husband had died recently, but she didn't mind being alone. He'd been a sailor in the merchant marine, anyway, so she'd spent most of her life waiting for him by the sea. They'd moved out here because when he retired, Dad told me, in a great example of his storytelling form, the desert was the closest thing the old sailor could find to open water. Dad had a soaring sympathy for such people, and the young Dana fit right in, Dana whose failing nerves and third bout with the measles so impaired his eyesight that, in 1834, he left Harvard at age 19 and shipped out for California.

In an archetypal romantic move, the wealthy Eastern boy signs up not as passenger (which he could've easily afforded) but as a common sailor—think again of feeble Theodore Roosevelt growing hard on a Wyoming ranch; pudgy, sensitive Frederic Remington out in Montana. "The change," Dana writes, "from the tight dress coat, silk cap and kid gloves of an undergraduate at Cambridge, to the loose duck trowsers, checked shirt and tarpaulin hat of a sailor . . . was soon made, and I supposed that I should pass very well for jack tar." Having sailed round the Horn, Dana first sets foot in California at Santa Barbara—in the surf, among

Hawaiians. "I shall never forget," he writes, "the impression which our first landing on the beach of California made upon me. The sun had just gone down; it was getting dusky; the damp night wind was beginning to blow, and the heavy swell of the Pacific was setting in, and breaking in loud and high 'combers' upon the beach." A boat from another ship, manned by "dusky Sandwich Islanders," rides past while Dana and the crew of his little boat sit scared outside the surf. The Hawaiians "gave a shout, and taking advantage of a great comber which came swelling in, rearing its head . . . they gave three or four long and strong pulls, and went in on top of the great wave." So Dana, like Twain but with more success, does as the Romans and surfs that rowboat ashore.

As he waits on the beach for the captain, Dana's eye returns to the waves, describing what sounds like a fine break: "the great seas were rolling in," he remembers, "in regular lines, growing larger and larger as they approached the shore, and hanging over the beach upon which they were to break, when their tops would curl over and turn white with foam, and, beginning at one extreme of the line, break rapidly to the other, as a long cardhouse falls when the children knock down the cards at one end." A shipmate remarks to Dana what you can bet he'd been delighting at himself: "Does not look much like Cambridge college, does it?" And to the beauty of the coast, Dana is quite alive: ashore at San Juan Capistrano, "there was a grandeur in everything around, which gave almost a solemnity to the scene: a silence and solitariness which affected everything! Not a human being but ourselves for miles; and no sound heard but the pulsations of the great Pacific! And the great steep hill rising like a wall, and cutting us off from all the world, but the 'world of waters!' " And it stirs in Dana "a glow of pleasure at finding that what of poetry I ever had in me, had not been entirely deadened by the laborious and frittering life I had led." How wonderful to know that someone who saw this coast in such undiminished beauty appreciated his good fortune. One of the constants in my own love of this coast has been an idle wish to have seen it before despoliation—it's hard, sometimes, to take Emerson's advice and believe that the world at its richest is honestly here before us.

But the heart of Dana's experience comes in San Diego, where twenty Sandwich Islanders live on the beach. Homesteading in an old Russian bread oven, they occupy themselves as one might expect: "in complete idleness—drinking, playing cards, and carousing in every way." (With all that free time and warm water, one feels safe assuming they used driftwood planks or felled trees as surfboards, or at least just bodysurfed.) And when Dana's captain tries to hire them, he has a timeless conversation with their spokesman:

> "What do you do here, Mr. Mannini?" asks the captain.
>
> "Oh, we play cards, get drunk, smoke—do anything we're a mind to."
>
> "Don't you want to come aboard and work?"
>
> "*Aole! aole make make mokou i ka hana*. Now, got plenty money; no good, work. *Mamule*, money *pau*—all gone. Ah! very good, work!—*maikai, hana hana nui!*"
>
> "But you'll spend all your money in this way," says the captain.
>
> "Aye! me know that. By-'em-by money *pau*—all gone; then Kanaka work plenty."

The ship then pulls out to visit other California ports, leaving Dana behind for a few months to cure hides and await its return. Imagine! This scion of a prominent Boston family spending an entire summer on the sands of San Diego only seven years after Jedediah Smith made the first white overland journey to California (and only three years after a band of Comanches surrounded Smith and killed him at a Kansas watering hole). Dana immediately hits it off with the islanders, who consider him the *Aikane* of the Kanakas—the white guy they can trust. "Here was a change in my life," Dana writes, "as complete as it had been sudden. In the twinkling of an eye, I was transformed from a sailor into a 'beach-comber' "—from student, to "jack tar," to beach bum. And among rough company, including "the most immense man that I had ever seen in my life," who had "been to sea from a boy, and had seen all kinds of service . . . merchantmen, men-of-war, privateers, and slavers." One of the Hawaiians, named for the missionary Hiram Bingham (who documented the decline of Hawaiian surfing), has had his two front teeth knocked out by his parents to show their grief over the death of King Kamehameha. Dana teases him that he lost the teeth eating Captain Cook, to which Bingham responds ominously that he was too young, but that his father was not.

Dana finds life on the beach indolent but eye-opening, among ships' crews of "half-breed" mestizos, Chilean Indians, blacks and mulattoes, Tahitians and Marquesan Islanders. Dana only mentions the whoring of others, but Lawrence Clark Powell reports that a letter came years later from a shipmate, wondering why Dana hadn't written of "the beautiful Indian Lasses, who so often frequented your humble abode in the hide house, and rambled through those splendid groves attached thereto, or the happy hours experienced rambling over those romantic hills, or sitting at twilight on those majestic rocks, with a lovely Indian Girl resting on your knee." This Puritan son gets what he always wanted: beach life as sex life, freedom. Think of young Herman Melville a few years later: *Typee*, his first South Seas narrative, opens when the young New Englander drifts into port in the Marquesas Islands after six months at sea. Playfully, even ironically, he remarks,

"What strange visions of outlandish things does the very name (Marquesas) spirit up! naked houris—cannibal banquets—groves of coca nut—coral reefs—tattooed chiefs—and bamboo temples; sunny valleys planted with bread-fruite trees—carved canoes dancing on the flashing blue waters—savage woodlands guarded by horrible idols—*heathenish rites and human sacrifices*."

A group of Marquesan girls swim out to the ship and climb aboard, "dripping with the brine and glowing from the bath, their jet-black tresses streaming over their shoulders, and half enveloping their otherwise naked forms." He describes the shock of the crew, and we can well imagine it, six months out of sight of land and hailing from frigid Nantucket. Melville admits that "our ship was now wholly given up to every species of riot and debauchery. Not the feeblest barrier was interposed between the unholy passions of the crew and their unlimited gratification." When it comes time to weigh anchor, Melville, not surprisingly, decides to jump ship. But after a few weeks, for Dana as for Melville, loneliness and fear of personal disintegration bring on homesickness. On Dana's last stopover in San Diego, a Hawaiian friend's dying of syphilis spooks Dana with the consequences of profligacy, and the whole sexy binge on the fringe of the Western world starts looking like a bad idea. As they turn toward home, he fixates on tales of white men degenerating among California's "mixed-blood" prostitutes and never returning home. So the coming-of-age excursion to the frontier doesn't include staying there; one sows one's oats, then settles back into one's proper place in society.

After sixteen months on the coast, Dana initially doesn't miss the place "universally called the hell of California," though he beams when a friend back in Boston Harbor sees him coming "down from aloft a 'rough alley' looking fellow, with duck trowsers and red shirt, long hair, and face burnt as black as an Indian's"—

a sailor and a savage, home from the territories. Historian Kevin Starr writes that at first Dana saw California as a detour from the proper path of his life, was consumed with doubts about both his wild life on the beach and his current one as an unhappily married lawyer. Perhaps to flog himself with his own passions, Dana took to cruising waterfront brothels dressed as a sailor, picking up prostitutes only to lecture them about their evil ways (one hopes they still requested payment). Later, increasingly unhappy in both marriage and the practice of law, he came to see those years in California as the best of his life. Returning to California twenty years later, Dana felt that "my life has been a failure compared with what I might and ought to have done."

Then, of course, there's Jack London, often referred to in surf writing as an example of the sport's great literary heritage. At the turn of that century, London does more to popularize Hawaiian surfing and California fun than anyone before or since. Life on his Sacramento Valley ranch getting tiresome, London stops over in the artists' colony at Carmel before the Pacific voyage that becomes *The Cruise of the Snark*. Monterey Bay becomes, in London's eyes, the Land of the Abalone Eaters, where painters, poets, and writers swim in the sea, gather shellfish, cheat on their spouses, commit suicide, and just generally live the California good life. In *The Valley of the Moon*, Jack London's salt-of-the-earth lead couple get their first sight of these bohemians when a blond beach boy, the Anglo Kanaka—"cherubic-faced, with a thatch of curly yellow hair . . . his body was hugely thewed as a Hercules"—sprints into the sea, "while above him, ten feet at least, upreared a wall of overtopping water . . . [he] sprang to meet the blow, and, just when it seemed he must be crushed, he dived into the face of the breaker and disappeared." Perhaps the first appearance of the California blond as Caucasian Natural Man. At a bohemian beach barbecue, London and the poet George

Sterling—kingpin of the scene and pen pal "Greek" to London's "Wolf"—dive for abalone while California writer Mary Austin, dressed like an Indian princess, swoons at the dusk.

London makes an unusual icon for surfers, however. Starr tells us that London "needed to think that he was a superman, one of Nietzsche's blond beasts . . . he had photographs made of himself in the seminude flexing his muscles, which he handed out to visitors." And all the while, it turns out, London detests exercise enough to have a valet tie his shoes every morning. Franklin Walker writes that Mary Austin found London those days "sagging a little with the surfeit of success"—eating, drinking, and smoking too much and always sick. Bad health ruins London's Pacific cruise on the *Snark*, his own version of Dana's and Melville's journeys to sea, so it's no surprise that the apparent virility of Hawaiian surfing gets London going. In "A Royal Sport for the Natural Kings of Earth," London ponders Natural Man at play, as a surfer rises "like a sea-god from out of the welter of spume and churning white . . . His black shoulders, his chest, his loins, his limbs—all [were] abruptly projected on one's vision." The native as everything the sickly and indolent London would so love to have been: "a Mercury—a brown Mercury. His heels are winged, and in them is the swiftness of the sea." When the wave is beaten into submission, and Kanaka steps ashore, "the pride in the feat shows in the carriage of his magnificent body as he glances for a moment carelessly at you who sit in the shade of the shore." Subduing the surf, Kanaka makes London swoon.

"But you are a man," London tells himself. ". . . Go to. Strip off your clothes that are a nuisance in this mellow clime. Get in and wrestle with the sea." Health, strength, nudity, and conquest, all by riding a wave—one surfing success with Alexander Hume Ford and George Freeth, and "From that moment I was lost," quite understandably. And an impressive triumvirate, very likely arranged by Ford. London writes of the session as though he just happened upon these two men among the waves, but it's hard to believe. As the consummate promoter of early Hawaiian tourism and publisher of the *Hawaiian Annual*, Ford would've known very well that showing the famous Jack London a good time would pay off in spades: London was being paid by the word for each of his serialized book chapters and was looking for material. And Ford couldn't have found a better water guide than Irish-Hawaiian Freeth, who was later hired by a southern California railway company to give local surfing demonstrations for precisely the same reason: in the hopes they would attract tourism. (Freeth actually made a great career as a California lifeguard and died quite young during a rescue.) Afterwards, London spends two days in bed (where he does most of his work anyway) with a horrible sunburn. "Upon one thing," he optimistically declares, "I am resolved: the *Snark* shall not sail from Honolulu until I, too, wing my heels with the swiftness of the sea, and become a sun-burned, skin-peeling Mercury." The cruise ends five years early because of London's horrible health, but not before he buys a few gifts for his beloved Sterling, his "male soul-mate." From the Solomon Islands, Walker reports, London writes "that he was bringing [Sterling] not only spears and war-clubs but the genitalia of a native female, 'a clitoris, dried with appurtenances,' duly strung up for an ear ornament."

5

I found out, over time, that the sea otter here at the Point, with his gray whiskers, black eyes, and powerful hands, preferred to dine on mussels and urchins, purple urchins like those in the tide pools among the rocks. Which was fine, given that urchins—spiky little spherical herbivores that they are—mow down kelp forests to leave kelp-free *urchin barrens*. And since kelp helps surf hold its shape by dampening out short-period wind chop and letting long-period groundswell roll through, the otter did more than scenic duty in making this place beautiful: he actually contributed to wave quality with every meal. The otter also occasionally ate crab, the purple rock crabs that lived in every little crevice like walking mouthfuls, but he didn't touch much else. Taking after the legendary Hawaiian surfer, waterman, and Olympic Gold Medal swimmer Duke Kahanamoku, I'd decided never again to eat shark—bad karma—but at a cedar-paneled sushi place I tried the otter's diet, with variations: urchin in nori over rice (textured much like pudding), crab in a California roll. I had a little wasabi and hot sake, of course, for that lovely, drippy-eyed sushi buzz, but ate the seafood as did the otter: sashimi. And when I considered his other options, things like turban snails, tube worms, and tunicates, I decided he had pretty good taste, though he missed out on clam and abalone and appeared not, as some local otters do, to hunt and kill large sea birds (cormorant, grebe, and gull had all been observed as prey).

On a drizzly dawn, I locked the truck near a deer that had been literally blown all over the highway in a terrifying, ghastly smear, as if made by an eighteen-wheeler at a hundred miles an hour. An enormous, blunt-headed owl loped across the carcass in its last hunt before light, then over the first brussels-sprout field torn up by the harvesters. Crossing the empty, silent road, I got that sweet, deserted-highway peace that makes you want to lie down and nap or do some stretching on the yellow line. But a young farm supervisor with no thumbs sat reading the newspaper nearby in his pickup, so I continued on my way, past two farmworkers hunched and bobbing down the rows, sprinkling something from buckets, silhouetted black against a flat gray sky. Full-grown sprouts still weighted the other fields, sage green and damp under the mist, and "Peligro/Poison" signs with skulls and crossbones stood along the dirt road warning of pesticide spraying the night before; permissible levels were apparently determined by average annual consumption, and as the basic human ate about one brussels sprout per year, they could saturate this place with chemical weapons. Since all the hemlock's tarlike, sticky death a few weeks ago, it had parched to a forest of broken stalks full of flitting sparrows; another autumnal death in the nadir of the year's growth cycle. High-tide surf washed quietly under the sound-dampening fog. Out at the Point, on an offshore rock, a family of harbor seals had taken up residence. As I changed in the half light, clouds pulled through the cypress and beaded on the grass and dirt. Someone's Coke can and soiled underwear lay in the open, and one of the seals let out a horribly displeased whine, the kind of predawn conversation that would give a sailor just cause for superstition. I felt somehow intrusive, as if eavesdropping on squabbling neighbors. I drank the last of my herbal tea and paddled out alone, watched long, warbled lines roll in out of the south. From a last South Pacific winter storm, these waves were yet another lingering vestige of summer, reflecting the very tilt of the earth in the angle of their approach. The first wave I caught was wound tight, bunched up, and glassy as I rose and fell with each bowl. The sky faded into a gray-blue as the fog began to break up, and eventually another man joined me. It was the older of those two friends, the one who always got so many waves. Off such a rocky and remote shore, this midmorning appearance implied far different motivation than idle fun in the sun. A week before, we'd had one laconic, surfer-jargon conversation that ended too soon when a few others paddled out. But I still wondered what he did for a living: somehow "surfer" just didn't suffice. Tradesman? Independently wealthy? He'd been distant at first, as we gave each other the requisite stern-faced nods. Sat side by side looking out to sea, not talking in spite of our solitude; one often does this while surfing, gives others a chance to be alone with their thoughts. Few people drive up here and make these walks out of a desire for company. He spoke a truncated English when I did try to chat.

"Fun ones, huh?" I said, offering a stock phrase as an opener.

"Tide's getting too low."

"When's the low?"

" 'Bout now," he said. Then he turned and paddled for a wave. The Point, I'd also discovered, had as daily regulars only this guy and a few others. He was by far the most dedicated, here every time I came and obviously at home. After a small but smooth wave, gentle turns and soft banks off the lip, we paddled back out together.

"All right," I said, fishing, "fess up. Trust fund? Unemployed?"

So many people *were* being laid off, with the economy turning down and construction all but halting. A lot of middle-aged guys were getting more waves than usual.

"Vince Collins," he offered, although I hadn't asked. Then he looked carefully at me and said he was a lecturer in math up at the university. He smiled a tight little grin, knowing why I'd asked, then laughed out loud and looked down at his board. "Pathetic," he said, "I know." His demeanor softened immediately, and I found out later this was typical of him—as much as he'd savagely berate the follies of other surfers and rant about smashing windshields and keying the cars of outsiders, it all melted to kindness in the face of another human.

Straight-edged little waves came clean and gray through the still rain with nobody to ride them but us two. Everything water—me, sea, air . . . him. Then he paddled away, suddenly but not frantically, just putting one hand in front of the other, head down. Nothing antisocial about this, although he certainly didn't encourage me to follow; one simply stayed alert, responded to the water, and kept moving. Seemed to me he was blowing it, though; most waves were hitting right where I was. In water, rise and fall makes a paced view: nothing from the troughs, the horizon from the peaks. A rill lifted him and he paddled over it, dropped out of sight behind. A bull kelp bulb the size of a grapefruit surfaced in the little boil in front of me—a medusan sea hag waving its long seaweed hair—and the otter floated on its back, wrapped in a kelp strand as a mooring against the current, little pointed ears catching the plunge of a pelican, the approach of a wave. Against the flat anvil-stone again on his belly, he smacked something new, a mussel perhaps (taking a big flavor risk). He reached high with his paw and smashed it down with a loud crack, then gnawed at it the way you'd crack a nut. Never seen him use anything but a stone, though otters are known to use soft-drink bottles to dislodge shellfish, to break open beer cans for resident octopi. A gull floated a few feet from him, upright and white against the gray water, waiting for scraps. The placid inner waters of the cove struck a surprising symmetry against the chaotic lines of land, like an Alpine lake below broken crags; water always an element that, like fire, one can watch endlessly.

Then I, too, rose with the rill and saw Vince, far off to my left, dropping into the biggest wave of the day, as if he'd *felt* it coming, didn't want to tip me off. After all, who knew how many there'd be? On his feet early, he took a high line, nothing fancy. He just moved from peak to trough and back again, arcing into the curl when the wall slowed down, stepping forward and trimming high when it sped up—the board an easy expression of unobtrusive desire. Many shortboarders—that is, riders of pointed boards under seven feet, as opposed to longboarders, riders of rounded boards over eight feet—ride as though glued in one stance. But Vince's style had been formed by a youth on the big longboards of the 1960s and the loose little twin-fins of the 1970s; he kept his feet in play, flicking the board about as much with his toes as with heavy weight shifts. I was cold and not surfing well, kept mistiming the suck and pitch, getting thrown headfirst. On my way down, I'd see Vince drop right in on the same wave, having politely watched and waited. In a long lull between sets of waves, through which surfers often sit silently, I mentioned how beautiful I thought the place was.

He looked at me a little askance, and for a moment I felt embarrassed at the sentiment. But then he smiled with surprise and looked behind us at the cliffs and hills.

"It's the most beautiful place on earth," he said quite seriously. "And I've had a look around." It only took him five minutes to get out that he was the first person to surf this place, that he'd been surfing here for thirty years, and that back then the reef had been quite different, much better. And best of all, there'd been nobody else here, ever: no fishermen, no weekend sunbathers, no mountain-bike geeks, and, most important, no surfers. "We used to park a mile up the highway," Vince said, "and walk down here just to throw off the Valleys. Only about ten guys even knew this place existed, and whenever some geek parked too close—this was in my wilder days—we'd smash their headlights and leave a note on the windshield telling them where to park and how to walk down here. We held on to this place five years longer by doing that, five more years before it finally got overrun." (I felt unclear about where I fit in, since I was obviously a recent arrival from inland, but his tone somehow included me in the camp of the good guys.) Back then, Vince said, the farmer still hadn't yielded a public right-of-way across his fields, but for some reason he'd liked Vince and often gave him rides in the back of his truck.

"You weren't here yesterday," Vince said suddenly, changing the subject. He took some mischievous pleasure in the announcement.

It had looked messy to me, much too windy, but I'd walked out anyway just to have lunch and watch the void shuffle around under the sun.

"Perfect in the morning," he said with a grin.

"Perfect?"

"Slaphappy."

"What?"

"Perfect."

We talked more between waves, with occasional lapses as we chased separate peaks—different parts of the reef causing distinct breaks quite near each other. Mostly we just floated, happy to sense some shared points of view. When I asked how he'd started surfing, he described what most surfers will: that first childhood moment of standing up on a board and knowing right then, with absolute certainty, that he was a surfer for life. He'd grown up in the 1950s in Chico, in the northern Central Valley, stealing cars and joyriding through cherry orchards, tow-surfing the irrigation canals by ropes tied to the bumpers. Back then Santa Cruz had been a low-budget summer destination for Central Valley families seeking to escape the stultifying valley heat. While the San Francisco country club set headed farther south to Carmel and Pacific Grove—London's and Sterling's haunts—the plebeians rode roller coasters and strolled the boardwalk. Once he'd picked up the surfing habit on a family trip, Vince and a few friends had taken to siphoning gas, stealing bottles to redeem for food money, speeding out to the coast. Maybe break into an empty beach house and have a little party. He apparently stole two hundred and fifty cars by the time he was a high-school senior, although it was all for kicks, and he never sold a single one of them. But he told all this without braggadocio, the way a sober alcoholic talks of drinking. He was just explaining how surfing, far from a bad influence, had slowed down his delinquency and put him on the right track. Now, presumably, he had a teacher's flexible schedule, a good pickup truck. And then, another set; Vince once again found his way to the right spot on the best wave and took off with a single paddle. Other sports so often require you to generate all the energy—one stares up at the inert mountain, laces up the running shoes—but surfing, however exhausting, is a system one plugs into.

The otter never came ashore, by the way. Otters can live their whole lives without coming to land, with fur four times as insulating as fat keeping them warm, buoyant, and waterproof. And they're quiet: no barking or baying like sea lions and seals; the otter just drifts alone, diving for food, staying in his small home range, tending his garden, holding a good feeding ground to court females. Otters are said to sleep curled up on the sand, paws over their noses, but this one did all his dozing among the slimy green patches of surface kelp (unless he beached elsewhere, along some cliff without enough sand for sunbathers or waves for surfers). He had the air of a nervous, irritated busybody, with none of the languid curiosity of a seal; but to be fair, he *did* have to eat a third of his body weight daily just to stay warm.

Then the fog pulled back, and for a while the view to sea could've been a winter stormscape, while the view immediately behind, to land, sparkled with bright blues and greens, leaving the late morning warm over the clearest water I'd seen. Ten feet down, grass waved among red algae and urchins, and the water tasted kelpy clean. Vince drifted away altogether when another fellow paddled out—being shy perhaps, or not gregarious enough to squander his attentions. The new surfer had a very northern European look to him: "Holland," he said, when I asked a little abruptly where he was from, "but I grew up in Liberia." He was happy to chat, and said his father did foreign development, still lived in Africa—had once seen a surfing picture in an airline magazine and decided he and his three boys ought to try it; on a stop-over in Spain he'd bought a couple of used boards. Then the Dutch surfer turned suddenly and paddled away—a good, shoulder-high wave—made a late drop, smacked the lip, and fell. Came up with a smile and paddled back out. "Well," he said, lying on his board, "we'd never even seen videos, much less the real thing. We just knew you caught waves and somehow ended up standing like the guy in the picture. It was hilarious." He said they got some better boards and a copy of *Surfer* magazine through a Pan Am steward whose circuit took him through California; they'd met him in a café in Monrovia, put in orders, and waited. Three months later he showed. "And there was this old Liberian man," he said, "a fisherman, who lived by the water and could predict swells. Not big storm swells, but local ones. He'd be like, 'There'll be waves tomorrow,' and he'd be right." So brothers and father had reinvented the surfing wheel, alone, in West Africa; now, scattered around the globe, they got together once a year—this year at a fabled left-point break in Tanzania. This brother now lived with his American wife in San Francisco, wondered if I was married. I mentioned my quasi girlfriend, now a graphic artist in San Francisco, and he asked if she surfed.

I just laughed, as would she have.

"You know," he said with great sincerity, "if she ever wants to try, I've got a brand-new, never-used foam board and a wetsuit that'd fit her."

"Never used at all, huh?"

"Nope."

"Wife's?"

"How'd you guess?"

An hour later, the Dutch surfer gone and Vince onshore changing clothes, I started paddling in; the otter looked up suddenly when I came too close, raised his silver-flecked head high out of the water to focus, then tucked the stone under one arm and dove. I dressed on shore and knew my toes were never going to dry out in this drizzle; even my T-shirt was damp. As Vince bent over to put on his pants, I noticed a tattoo on his butt, leaned a little closer to make the thing out, then realized it was like one of those tailgating bumper stickers: IF YOU CAN READ THIS, YOU'RE TOO CLOSE.

"If someone asks," Vince said suddenly, standing up, "what I've done with my life, what'll I say? Surfed the Point and taught math?" He shook his head with a laugh. "Raw mediocrity." It didn't, of course, strike me that way, and I wanted to tell him but couldn't think how. I also wanted to ask if I could meet him surfing some time, maybe share the drive; but I knew it was too soon. The fog now well offshore, and fingers of wind printing deep-blue splotches on the light-blue sea, we started back and I got to wondering about a culture that marked his life that way, a man who'd mastered a skill he deeply loved, learned to truly know an element. On campus, he explained as we walked, boards under our arms, he had to lie about irregularities of schedule, fabricate false travel itineraries for sabbaticals; the frivolous aura of surfing having invalidated the great achievement of his life. No social cachet at all—just a guy who couldn't grow up. And then the oddest thing happened: a cougar stood in the road, a hundred yards off, its long, supple tail swinging slowly from side to side. As we walked closer, it stepped into the dead hemlock on the side of the road, looked back out with its brown head, and then disappeared. As we approached the point where the cat had entered the brush, Vince suggested that the petting-zoo concept might not be appropriate, thought we ought to give the beast a little room. We stepped off the far side of the road, and as we came even with the bush, Vince said, "Is that it? There it is, right?"

Ten feet away, waiting under a willow: a cat the size of a very large dog, a wild thing on a scale quite different from the raptors and their rodents. We both froze. And suddenly it vanished like a ghost—unafraid, unhurried. One second it lay watching, the next it was gone. None of the coyote's slinking or the deer's bolting. A visitation in a backwater place, all part of the wet skin and salty eyelashes, draining sinuses and muscles loose in the way only water can make them. We were both stunned, and Vince said that in thirty years he'd never seen a cougar before. Big predators change your whole sense of an ecology: sharks in the water, lions on the land, a hawk overhead.

"By the way," Vince said, as we walked back up the path, "get a new surfboard." A few hippie farming interns stood smiling in the field, having fun—not, after all, getting paid.

"Because of the lion?"

"No, because you need one." Surfboard shape changes constantly in a blend of technical advancement and fashion; Vince made a point of eschewing whatever the current trend. At the moment, the young pros had made wafer-thin little blades the craze; Vince told me to steer clear of that baloney, get something with a little heft. "Nobody in their right mind rides one of those ridiculous potato chips," he said, "but as long as they do, guys like you and me will paddle circles around them, which is fine." As we got our last glimpse of ocean, Vince said an evening surf was out of the question.

Why? How could he tell? The winds seemed right, plenty of swell . . .

"Color—wind'll be onshore." The gradations in the ocean's blue had tipped him off; not genius, but an intimate knowledge of place, an eye adapted to particular minutiae. Still, nothing learned, gained, or earned in a public way, just his secret discipline, his private pleasure.

6

Vince's suggestion led to my discovering another surfing peculiarity: off-the-rack boards cost more, generally speaking, than custom boards. Many serious surfers simply don't buy boards out of shops; they develop a relationship with a particular shaper in their town and have every board made slightly differently in an ongoing search for the perfect combination of elements. The endless play with length, thickness, bottom contour, outline curve, fin placement, and other considerations gives the surfer, over time, a phenomenally complex relationship to his tool. Even more peculiar is that there is no substantial price difference between the very best and the very worst boards: they all use largely the same materials in largely the same amounts. Longboards cost more than shortboards, but good longboards don't cost much more than lousy ones, and likewise for shortboards. There's simply no such thing as a "starter" model and a "top of the line" model; no deluxe edition with loads of expensive extras, no latest high-tech pricey material or heat treatment. There are boards better suited for learning, others better for tube riding or big waves, but the *quality* distinction is quite subtle and subjective.

Tom Blake, in his 1935 *Hawaiian Surfriders*, explains the way it used to be in the islands: the commoner's nine-foot *alaia* board, for *kakala*, a curling, deadly wave; and the nobleman's eighteen-foot *olo* board, for *opuu*, a gentle roller. One chose a tree—hardwood breadfruit for the *alaia*, porous wiliwili for the *olo*—then placed an offering of red *kumu* fish at the trunk, cut down the tree, dug a hole in the root, and left the fish there with a prayer. Then one chipped the trunk with a stone adze until a board emerged; corrugated coral helped smooth out the adze marks, and a paint made from *mole-ki* root and burned kukui nuts gave it a glossy finish. Burying the board in mud sealed the wood pores, and a last rubbing with oil gave it a final polish. Stateside, into the 1920s, the surfboard was still a six- to nine-foot flat-bottomed piece of solid redwood: one bought a plank at the lumberyard, chopped it into shape with an ax, and whittled it down with a knife. Three and a half inches thick and over a hundred pounds, with no fin or keel. Tom Blake's own 1926 hollow boards came next. Blake had grown up in Wisconsin, spent his first few years after high school hoboing on freight trains, and eventually landed in Los Angeles. There, with no formal training, he set the world record in the open ten-mile swim and eventually designed his revolutionary boards: long, closed canoes, beautiful pieces of maritime architecture designed largely for open-water paddling races. Then, in 1934, two southern Californians got sick of "sliding ass" while trying to carve turns on faster waves. C. R. Stecyk writes in *The Surfer's Journal* that the two went home after a frustrating session, hacked the rear of the plank into a V, and sanded it smooth—soon they were working their wooden slabs into gorgeously organic, curved hulls with keels carved into the bottom shape.

The next big leaps in surfboard design came, Stecyk writes, during the Second World War, from a young man named Bob Simmons who was unfit for military service because of a left arm damaged in a bicycling accident. Simmons remains one of the sport's oddest heroes: brother of a very successful inventor and a high-school dropout with total recall, he tested into Caltech and performed extraordinarily, going on to work as a machinist and eventually as a mathematician for Douglas Aircraft. During the lean war years—few people on the beaches, gasoline and tires tightly rationed—Simmons also took to hopping freight cars at the Pasadena rail yard, riding the coast looking for waves. Quitting his mathematician's job when the surf came up, getting rehired when it dropped, he eventually gutted a 1937 Ford flatbed to put in a mattress and camping supplies, mixed in a little kerosene to stretch his mileage. Surfers were already shaping boards out of balsa, but it took this mathematician and trained engineer to understand the technological advances offered by military war research. Simmons used a U.S. naval report on planing hulls to apply research on aspect ratio—the ideal balance of length to width, developed in aircraft wing design—to his surfboards. He also took the report's recommendation on the strengthening of planing hulls with fiberglass. Styrofoam had been used in the war as well, for fuselage radar domes, and by 1947 Simmons was pouring his own foam in a backyard mold and laminating it with fiberglass. Stecyk writes that Simmons integrated the new materials and hull designs with military research on the dynamics of waves, originally meant to aid in amphibious landings. The results were what Simmons called his "hydrodynamic planing hulls," boards faster and much easier to control than their predecessors. He was killed in 1954 in big surf at Windansea, but his boards are still coveted artifacts.

Until the late 1960s, boards were ten to eleven feet long and four inches thick; by the early seventies they were in the seven-foot range. The old longboard style has a wonderful grace to it: on a stable, heavy board, your feet are in constant play up and down its length, stepping back to stall, forward to speed, planting a foot in the rear to weight a turn, then scampering up to hang your toes off the front. The great old longboard moves revolved partly around classic postures—a static elegance—and partly around the loose, walking, casual cool of nose riding. The new shortboard style is geared more to fast, slashing turns, a kind of aggressive gymnastic. Design variations also become, over time, increasingly precise and arcane. The obvious considerations are length and width, both of which affect volume and therefore flotation. The better a board floats, the faster it will paddle, and the faster it paddles, the better it will catch waves; but at higher speeds, extra bulk will make the board plane on top of the water rather than carve through it, compromising control. Other differences lie in side rail shape (where and to what degree the curve of the board's edge becomes a hard angle), the location of the board's widest point, and the extent of its lengthwise flat spot. Tail shape is also crucial: a stiletto-pointed pin tail will keep the center point of the board close to the wave, holding a high, fast line on a steep wave; a wide, flat-bottomed tail will give the board a loose, broad pivot for skateboardlike sudden turns. Still finer distinctions lie in the contours of the board's underside—distinctions that can be difficult to make out visually. A shaper can build very subtle convex or concave areas running the board's length, channeling the water's flow for particular effects.

In 1994, the Beach Lifestyle Industry Group reported that 310,000 surfboards were sold in the United States, and yet not a single large producer dominates the market. While a few Australian and southern California shapers sell their boards worldwide, it is primarily a cottage industry, and every little surf town has its local shaper or two, guys with a shop in their garage and a loyal following. So, heeding Vince's advice, I made an appointment with his shaper across town at Ocean Groove Surfboards—an old garage on a shady, cottage-lined street of redwoods and wispy, scented eucalyptus. Jack Bence, a journeyman carpenter who'd finally committed to shaping full-time, was an underground big-wave hero with sound local credentials; he'd been surfing the Lane for twenty years but could also talk Pipeline, Grajagan, Jeffrey's Bay. Vince had recommended him highly. Jack bought his house back before the market blew and had put in yellow roses and a Japanese rock garden. Loose-limbed in jeans and an old chinchilla jacket, hair full of foam dust, he stood in his garage with the door up, a beer open, a game on the radio. When I parked and stepped into the windless fog, he pulled off his face mask and shook my hand; then he took a sheet of paper from a box. He asked questions like a therapist with a new client: "How do you surf?"

"I don't know," I said. "I mean, I've only been surfing a few years, but I want to shred, you know? Not just cruise."

"Where do you surf?" He looked right at me as he asked, and I noticed deep crow's feet, smile wrinkles by his mouth—time spent in sun and salt. His hands were surprisingly delicate.

"Up north," I said, trying to sound bored, "town when it's huge."

He wrote a note, appeared to make a tough decision. Along the wall hung photographs of pretty women and deep, sucking tubes.

"So you don't get out in the big stuff?" he asked.

"Huh?" What a question! "Ahhh . . . no, I mean, pretty big. Double overhead, I guess. Maybe bigger, sometimes."

He nodded and wrote down a few numbers.

"Where do you want to take your surfing?"

"Floaters, aerials . . . I mean, I'm twenty-seven, and I know that's old, but I grew up skateboarding so I want to rip."

He nodded as if to say, Yes, my son, this is healthy. "So . . . lot of tail rocker?"

Three more unfiberglassed boards hung from a rack, each with an airbrushed pattern drying: flames, a sunburst, a naked woman of exaggerated proportions.

"Rocker? Well, my seven-two projects me too parallel to the lip. I need something I can smack it square with. So . . ."

"You want to watch me start?"

Through his shop, past foam blanks—raw surfboard forms piled along the walls—to a partitioned room at the back of the garage. In the black-walled cubicle, a seven-foot blank rested flat on a stand. Along the walls were waist-high fluorescent strips to throw subtle curves into shadowed relief. With a power planer connected to a vacuum hose, Jack skinned the blank quickly into a thing distinct and sharp in its form. Wearing expensive basketball shoes, he walked up and down the length of the board like an old ballroom dancer. Then he picked up a long piece of plywood, a curve template that would determine the arc of the board's outline. He traced one onto the rear of the board, another toward the nose, then cut them out with a handsaw, again walking the length of the board in a steady sweep. The subtleties of bottom shape and rail curve went in with still more walking, passing strips of sanding gauze across each part of the board, never making a change that he didn't carry all the way through the board's shape. And although he made many measurements, followed lines and marks and patterns, he also paused several times to turn the board upright and run his hands down its length. Then he'd flip it back onto the stand to smooth something, fix an irregularity. Back and forth from the measured to the felt in a fast, physical rendering of a complex of theories and desires, running through a kata of moves that rendered a unique, functional sculpture with a life of its own. On the wall, a graffito: "Yes, Grasshopper, now that you have learned to laminate, you may begin to sand."

He stopped eventually for a break, said he had the basic outline in place and would fine-tune later. So we stepped back into the garage, and I asked him again about the overall shape.

"Oh, pretty basic," he said. "Enough tail rocker to let you come real vertical off the bottom. Pretty flipped-up nose'll be nice on late drops, and I gave you a rounded squash tail so it'll feel pretty loose, but it should hold a big turn just fine. Little extra thickness under your chest'll give you some paddling, but I domed it down to pretty nimble rails, so it's not a cork at all. Also, I generally do a single to double concave in the bottom, but it's real subtle."

Sounded good.

7

As a paying, full-price customer—and thus in no way an insider—I could be assured that delivery of my board would be at the bottom of Jack's schedule. But an idle surfer has plenty to think about, like sharks: naturally, one takes an interest in them, studies photographs of their gaping, bloody mouths—prostrate on the decks of fishing boats or on municipal piers, great whites always seem a ghastly and naked smear of triangular teeth and pale, fleshy gums. And when stared at all afternoon, the stuffed great white at the San Francisco Aquarium—thirteen feet long and somewhat deflated in its freezer case—serves reasonably well as an embodiment of one's relationship to fate: you know they're out there, you even know they're more likely to be at one place than another, and, yet, the odds are on your side. You either quit surfing (unthinkable), or accept a sentiment commonly shared in the water: "Yeah, I figure, if a shark's going to eat me, he's going to eat me." Sensible enough, although one feels compelled to ask how many aspects of late-twentieth-century American life involve the possibility of being devoured by a two-thousand-pound predator with razor teeth. A kid I knew in high school had once seen coroner's photographs of a Monterey surfer bitten almost in half—he repeatedly told me how most of the man's rib cage was gone and how his organs spilled across the table. The board had beached first, with a classic cookie-cutter bite missing; the body drifted in the cold currents for nearly two weeks before it was found. Years later, another local man was having a great time at a remote reef when he felt as if someone had dropped a VW on his back—suddenly he was underwater facing a huge eye. And in Oregon, a shark bit the board out from under a surfer who was sitting in wait for a wave; that awful mouth surged up and chomped onto the fiberglass between his legs. The shark bolted with the board in its teeth, dragging the surfer along by the ankle leash; when the shark turned to charge, the surfer grabbed its tail—two other surfers witnessed this—and they wheeled around in circles together before it let go.

There were whole weeks that fall when the Point was no good; I'd even walked out the dirt road several times in the rain, as if visiting a lover never quite in the mood. Somehow Vince and his friend, whose name was Willie Gonzales, were never even checking it on those days, having apparently predicted its conditions through remote observations. But that's one of the sport's mysteries: one must be available, flexible, always in shape. A storm could break for one day and produce the greatest four hours your reef has seen in a decade, only to pick up the next and blow the waves apart. One comes to welcome serendipity into the patterns of daily life, accept the fleeting nature of happiness, and avoid all unnecessary time constraints. But even when I could find waves, the cold occasionally felt like a kind of oppressive duty; sometimes I wanted to just hide indoors, drink some hot tea. On one such stormy afternoon, I took coffee and a big Toll House cookie (my unqualified favorite food) over to the Santa Cruz Surf Museum at the lighthouse for a look at the obligatory chewed-up board. A small room with the air of a temple, the museum had a historical range of boards hung all over the walls, from redwood planks to the latest big-wave elephant guns. Old black-and-white photographs showed smiling boys in simpler times; an older gentleman wearing a satin Santa Cruz Longboarders Association jacket mentioned that the winter of '41 was a beaut. And then I found it: huge teeth had crunched the fiberglass like a potato chip, tangible evidence of a phantom reaper, like the footprints of a yeti or film footage of a ghost. A glass case held photographs of Erik Larsen, the victim, in bed, with heavily bandaged arms; handwritten doctor's reports described deep lacerations and massive blood loss. Pieces of wetsuit, also behind glass, looked as if they'd been shredded by a tree mulcher. A photo caption compared territorial bites to feeding bites, said Larsen was slated for dinner. Expecting fatty seal meat instead of fiberglass and neoprene, lean muscle and bone, sharks usually spit surfers out; but the one that got Larsen had come back for a second bite.

Still, tide dropping, big storm on the way and time wasting, I said my mantras—"more likely to be killed by a drunk driver, more likely to be struck by lightning"—and drove north. All the way up the coast, I felt the dread of true wilderness, of getting an upward view in the food chain—something humans have worked hard at avoiding, like exposure to the elements and procreative sex. I changed into my wetsuit with a little reggae on the tape deck: "Kill de white man, kill de white man . . ." On the path, panicked cottontails scampered into the dead hemlock as I passed. I paddled out in water slate-gray and disappointingly flat, caught a little nothing of an ankle-high wave, then drifted about and took comfort in the water's murkiness—concentrated on surfaces, ignored the way my legs faded down into the milky green. Smelled the brine, watched granite-colored light wave along the still outer waters. There's a rare quality of sun and shade here on cloudy days, with the dramatic contrasts of black-and-white film. Sunbeams hit a patch of outer sea with glaring intensity, the water so bright against the black distance as to appear shivering and splashing in response to the light. Vince was nowhere to be seen, hadn't been for a few days. I rose and fell a little, lying down, eyes at water level. Ishmael again: "These are the times of dreamy quietude . . . when beholding the tranquil beauty and brilliancy of the ocean's skin, one forgets the tiger heart that pants beneath it; and would not willingly remember, that this velvet paw but conceals a remorseless fang." Willie Gonzales drifted far outside, arms folded, watching the shifts in shadows and holding a kelp strand as an anchor against the current. A seal's shiny head surfaced quietly behind him, undetected. It watched Willie's back for a minute, then leapt out of the water and came down with a terrific slap: thrashing and kicking, Willie spun around on his board, utterly hysterical, face white, screaming, "What was that!? What the *hell* was that!?"

And I didn't blame him: you can think you're thinking only about the super chicken burrito you intend to have for lunch, brush your leg against a thick boa kelp stalk and absolutely flip with terror, find that death by devouring lurks just a thought below your mind's surface. *Sharkiness*: state of mind spoken as a state of place—"Getting kinda sharky out here, dontcha think?" —a combination of a break's history, water depth, and exposure to open ocean, maybe crowd level, fog density, and even just sheer distance from the highway. I paddled over to a patch of kelp to hide from the deep, and, thinking of the guy who'd been dragged around, sat up to avoid decapitation. A neighbor of mine had been sitting on his board near here just recently, thinking what a drag it would be if a shark appeared. There were so few waves, he'd have had to paddle in. And just then, he'd seen a four-foot dorsal fin ten feet away from him, a huge, swirling wake displacing as it moved slowly past. He told me his eyes couldn't quite process it at first, kept trying to see a seal or a sea lion; but then another surfer had *leaned* around the fin and nodded frantically with an expression that said, *Uh huh, that's exactly what you think it is!* As they paddled for the beach, my neighbor turned around once to see the fin slowly following; decided right then not to look back again. When they'd screamed the other surfers ashore, one diehard remained in the water, unbelieving. I had actually mistaken a sea-lion flipper for a fin once and discovered a peculiar human dynamic: guys want to scorn your misplaced fear, are ever ready to laugh at he who cries wolf, but never quite do. The danger is simply too legitimate for teasing. Nearly everyone, no matter how gruff and grim, is scared witless at the thought of being torn apart while conscious, of watching a spreading slick of one's own blood. Nevertheless, Skinny once felt convinced he'd seen a great white inside a wave: he'd paddled for shore and left without telling any of the other ten surfers in the water, didn't want to be ridiculed. But great whites were, after all, nowhere more common than right here on this coast. The patch of ocean from Monterey, just south of where I floated, out to the Farallon Islands off San Francisco and north to Bodega Bay just north of the Golden Gate had become known—in wonderfully oblique terms—as the Red Triangle. And, indeed, I'd been out alone at the Point one morning at just the hour when several surfers sighted a great white less than a mile north.

So many disturbing traits, once you look into them—with a somewhat morbid curiosity, I'd begun prowling around the University Science Library, an airy new building with gestures toward native construction materials, a self-conscious sensitivity to the surrounding redwoods, and the rational and antiseptic calm of too many quantitative minds padding silently down well-carpeted corridors. A few tidbits: sharks are the world's only known *intrauterine cannibals*; as eggs hatch within a uterus, the unborn young fight and devour each other until one well-adapted predator emerges. (If the womb is a battleground, what then the sea?) Also, without the gas-filled bladders that float other fish, sharks, if they stop swimming, sink. This explains their tendency to lurk along the bottom like twenty-one-foot, 4,600-pound benthic land mines with hundred-year life spans. Hard skin bristling with tiny teeth sheathes their flexible cartilage skeletons—no bone at all. Conical snouts, black eyes without visible pupils, black-tipped pectoral fins. Tearing out and constantly being replaced, their serrated fangs have as many as twenty-eight stacked spares (a bite meter embedded in a slab of meat once measured a dusky shark's bite at eighteen tons per square inch). And all of the following have been found in shark bellies: a goat, a tomcat, three birds, a raincoat, overcoats, a car license plate, grass, tin cans, a cow's head, shoes, leggings, buttons, belts, hens, roosters, a nearly whole reindeer, even a headless human in a full suit of armor. Swimming with their mouths open, great whites are indiscriminate recyclers of the organic—my sensitive disposition, loving family and affection for life, my decent pickup, room full of books, preoccupation with chocolate in the afternoons, and tendency to take things too personally: all immaterial to my status as protein.

Leftovers from premammalian times, survivors of the dinosaur extinction, sharks evolved completely and always in the sea, never in fresh water. First appearing 350 million years ago, they've descended from sixty-foot, fifty-ton prehistoric monsters, truly overdetermined predators—in one photo a group of scientists stands comfortably inside a pair of fossilized jaws. Great whites are capable of between forty and seventy knots—calculated from photographic blur—and one writer describes a diver in the Mediterranean being hit so hard he exploded. Another mentions a white shark leaping clear out of the water to pull a seal off a rock, and writes that "in most attacks, witnesses see neither seal nor shark, only a sudden explosion blasting spray fifteen feet high, then a slick of blood on the surface." One never sees the white before it strikes, no speeding fin: it surges up in ambush, jaw distended, and tears out fifty-pound chunks of flesh. Death coming truly like a stroke of lightning; in that vast, three-dimensional world of the sea, the surfer's world is quite two-dimensional, all surface and shore, with neither depth nor open sea. Aiding the shark's stealth are jelly-filled subcutaneous canals on its head and sides that are lined with neuromasts called ampullae of Lorenzini, a kind of prey radar detecting faint electrical fields. (As a surfer waits for a wave, his very life force pulses like a homing beacon.) And their powerful eyes—with optic nerves thick as ropes—see detail quite poorly, are adapted only to separating prey from background. Among the world's most efficient predators, great whites have a kill rate better than ninety percent, while the hawks just inland strike all day without luck.

I popped a kelp bulb just as a seal rose and looked at me, processing my presence. Perhaps wondering why I'd be stupid enough to dress like him in this part of town.

"Don't like seeing seals," said a surfer nearby.

Now I was nervous, having always seen seals as good news.

"Just paranoid," he answered, when I asked why, "because . . . I'm Erik Larsen." He sounded almost apologetic.

I looked closely, saw the resemblance to the bandaged figure in the photographs. He rolled up his wetsuit sleeve to show deep scars the length of his forearm; I let a little wave pass—had to ask.

"Kind of foggy out there," he said, telling a much-told tale, "and my brother had just gone in. I got this weird feeling a big animal was under me. Really hoping it was a sea lion. Then I saw teeth, like coming up at me."

Willie drifted over to listen.

"And then my whole leg was in the thing's mouth," Larsen said, slouching like a beaten veteran. "It cut my thigh muscle in half and severed my femoral artery." He looked outside at a three-wave set; clouds still a gray continuum. Willie said he'd heard you bled to death if your femoral artery got cut.

"If you slit it, you do," Larsen said, "but it's like a rubber band, so if you cut it all the way like mine, it'll snap back and close a little."

Not a distinction I enjoyed picturing. Willie looked toward the beach.

Larsen explained how the shark let go, circled, and attacked again, this time at his head. "I put up my arms," he said, crossing them before his face, "and it cut all the adductor tendons and my right brachial artery—the really big one under your bicep. My arms were all flopping around in its mouth. Yeah, I totally remember thinking how much room there was in there, like plenty for me. But I got one arm out and hit it in the eye."

He took a breath. I was stunned, couldn't be patient—and then?

"It let go," he said. "And I actually got on my board. No shit. And the miracle is, I could even paddle because I still had the tendons that pulled down, even though it cut the ones that lift up. I actually caught a wave." He laughed a little. "Yeah, a little one. Belly-rode it in, and a lady came out with her kid and I told them how to tie tourniquets. When the chopper got there I'd lost a third of my blood."

The end of the story left an awkward silence: what to say? Larsen stroked into a waist-high right and surfed it casually, did what the wave wanted. I floated awhile alone, then caught one in—waves kind of small, not real interesting.

8

That storm thrashed the north coast for nearly a week, swelled the rivers to chocolate-brown torrents full of uprooted trees, rotting mattresses, and the invisible hazards of septic seepage. Which was just fine: I needed time to forget about Whitey, old *Carcharodon carcharias* out there with the big fin. But even in the rain, I walked each morning to the cliff by my house to survey the domain, and usually found Vince doing the same. He lived in my neighborhood, it turned out, and rode a bike down daily at dawn. He'd stand with binoculars while his wife slept, integrate the color of the outer bay waters with apparent wind and swell directions, tidal swings with his class schedule, and formulate a plan. I began timing my own cliff strolls around his, often keeping an eye out my bedroom window for him; when I saw him pedal past, I'd pull on a hooded sweatshirt, grab a thermo-mug of Tension Tamer herbal tea, and scramble along for a chat. He had an encyclopedic knowledge of the entire county's surf spots, thirty years' worth of experiential data on over a hundred breaks in every imaginable set of conditions; he also hated crowds and did everything in his power to avoid surfing in them. In fact, he often just wished me well on my day's search and left with a quiet smile, apparently off to an esoteric break he didn't feel ready to bestow upon me.

The second day of that storm was one such time, and for lack of any known alternative I drove to the Point alone—sun low and sky broken with black and white clouds, northern horizon utterly dark. As I slowed to park, I saw Willie jump out of his classic El Camino just in time to save a half-blind little dog from a produce truck. We both recognized it as local and carried it out with us, along the muddy road, among the soggy, dead hemlock and the oxalis sprouting in the empty seed rows. Willie and I hadn't spoken much before, just "Hey, now" in the water. Something very refined about his manner and speech, including the linguist's joy with which he played at surf talk. A well-heeled friend of his, he told me as we strolled, had recently subscribed to a service called Wave Fax that zapped him a daily analysis of every possible global storm pattern that could send surf our way; today's sheet apparently called for a big northwest swell in the next few days, some storm stalled over British Columbia. I'd been surfing the Point almost daily—even when it wasn't ridable—just for the pleasure of being there. Aside from Vince, I saw nobody there more often than Willie. Medium height, very thin and lithe, with high cheekbones, a strong jaw and dark eyes, he always seemed at once sardonic and gently bemused, his spidering crow's feet more suggestive of a lifetime of thoughtful grins than of any abiding pain. Willie had a clever, chatty way about him, but he was also quite private and one didn't ask prying questions. Although he looked very much the yuppie surfer in a sharp Patagonia wind shell, Ray•Ban sunglasses, jeans, and bright-yellow rain boots, Willie apparently lived quite nearby, rented a studio on a farm in the hills above. The path we walked was thick with fresh blades of grass and early mustard sprouts; a few swallows dove and chirped—the point being, finally, to just *see*. Not that this was pristine wilderness—even our lovely wild mustard couldn't claim true local status—but I clung to the transcendentalist's insistence that the golden age *had* to be now, the world *had* to be available for audiences today. If it wasn't, well . . . you know. So rows of chaos like the little strip up the dirt road, the bands of uncultivated earth between fields and alongside the railroad tracks, had to promise enough change to merit watching over time.

And from the cliff, we saw twenty dolphins in two pods move among the breakers—crowds of sharp little black fins, arcing and diving. A plume of spray, tiny from afar, shot up in the western blue: the first of the migrating gray whales passing south. As we changed, a clear light broke through the clouds across a glassy, storm-thrown sea. There was no wind, but everywhere was its evidence; that Arctic low pressure's waves hadn't yet organized, still reflected the gale's chaos without the ordering pull of surface tension, gravity, and time. The waves had a warping, organic feel, as if unchained from the demands of reef and swell; cold, ten-foot peaks rolled in and lurched over unpredictably. Long, nutty drops with the rear foot back to keep the nose up, turning high, trimming before the curl over a foam-covered surface, knees buckling over bumps of chop. So odd to leave such pastoral calm for such roaring, un*earth*ly wilderness. And then, paddling back out in the calm between sets: surfboard rising and falling over and through the shiny seas; eyes just off the water as rills and unallied little peaks came and went. The horizon appeared, vanished, tilted, dropped; granitic Pacific and precipitant sky uniform and still. Far outside floated four black figures in black hoods, hunched-over mendicants cowering before the ropy rain beards that fingered the bright gray distance.

A small blond man named Steve, another quasi regular, talked loudly between waves about being laid off, feeling desperate, maybe moving back to New York. He'd quit a good job digging wells for a better one at a perfume plant; turned out the perfume put him in bed, sick for a week, and it was too late to go back to the wells. Now, nobody was hiring at all; he'd been walking up to building job sites for a month. His wife had lost patience, was tired of supporting him. He spoke mostly to Willie, though they'd never formally met. This swirling cove was just the closest thing Steve had to a corner pub, and Willie our closest thing to a bartender. Steve sounded pretty spooked, kind of stopped surfing and rambled for a while about how he didn't know what the hell to do. VA said they'd match any salary he could get, but employers didn't care. Willie's empathy seemed very real, as if he'd lost enough times not to take any recent victories personally.

The squall again upon us, a downpour started as distinct, visible drops splashing alone, rippling and subsiding on the oily surface; then it poured, and the water became an electric buzz and jump, the whole surface shivering, alive, a nexus now between water falling and fallen: no reflectivity at all, and the rain seemed to hold down the sea, press its coarseness into even forms. Shaking in my wetsuit—permeable second skin interfacing between flesh and brine—I hunkered down and waited, looked across a desert of undulating, fuzzy green water dunes and saw, suddenly, a gargantuan sentry, a massive, blunt black head just inside the peak. The big, dark face of a sea lion startled me almost off my board—a seven-foot, six-hundred-pound seal with a mane, swimming alone in the off-season, between matings and moltings, far north of the rookery where the females and pups lingered, foraging for squid, halibut, rockfish. Aleutians, I'd read, made much use of them, skins for boat coverings and waterproof clothing, meat for food, fat for fuel. Sea lions are also said to be playful, to chase and catch their own air bubbles for kicks, and are the classic circus seals—balancing wine glasses on their noses while going down stairs, clapping at their own performances. But this one loomed up so quickly, so out-of-scale, it suggested all that invisible space below, that world of enormous creatures close by and unseen. Then it held its black, pupilless eyes open to my light and dove.

A sudden, violent wind blew ribbons of mist twisting off wave backs like spindrift in a blizzard. Shivering, ice-cream headaches and a sore shoulder from overuse—as I paddled into a wave, the wind spray in my face was like a fire hose and the ride felt like off-roading, bouncing across bending bands of chop. Then the rain let up and the cliffs appeared again; the farmers had plowed under all the sprout stalks, and the soil—paled slightly from a few days' wind—was again drenched and black. In the respite, a soft-spoken redheaded surfer chatted about backpacking into California's remote Lost Coast, up near the Oregon border. They'd ridden twelve-foot waves, with seals everywhere and even the occasional killer whale. From Malibu, he'd moved up here for country-style surf, thought he'd just keep drifting north as the years went by, looking for elbow room. He saved rent while attending the university by living in a tent in the forest behind campus; he and his girlfriend, a beautiful and lanky tomboy surfer/skater, had been in the forest together for the last two years straight. Right through the rains without a problem.

And there was the sea lion again, absurdly large. A nineteenth-century ship's captain describes hunting sea lions here during the Gold Rush—how his sailors got between a beached herd and the water, shouting and waving weapons to cause panic. A bull resisted and got a musket ball through the brain, a lance in its mouth. Then the sailors charged. Panicked lions climbed over each other as they were butchered, shed famous quantities of blood (its excess allowing for extended dives without breathing). The sailors then flayed the lions on the blood-soaked beach and peeled off the thick blubber, hauled it to the ship for boiling. And down this particular sea lion went, its long back a slick organization amid the foam and roar. A truly transitional life, theirs, not at all pelagic: on a steep, rocky shore, sea lions will leap from waves onto high ledges, use the backwash to get out again. And even in their slovenly living habits, they are quite liminal: sharing breeding grounds with cormorants even as ravens and foxes scavenge their food scraps. Gulls are said to walk freely among sea lions on beaches, even to peck feces from a pup's anus or descend in a flock to fight over a fresh placenta.

But still, the size and speed of the one I'd seen today were unsettling: a blackness within the foamy green of a wave, shooting submerged before the curl. For an instant the ghost form surfed the wave's internal curves—subsurface reflections of the visible waves above—and then it vanished. Perhaps he'd seen our play, recognized it as his own; they are known to bodysurf in groups, returning again and again to a good peak. Even their love lives are at once familiar and strange, as territorial bulls fight for good breeding spots along the water, space themselves along rocks where waves can wet them and clean off carcasses. Females, far outnumbering the males, cluster around the bulls and love each other's company. And for all that bull biting and posturing, the females—who do all the sexual selecting anyway—ignore male territories, wander freely about the beach. A couple of weeks after birthing, a female's vulva again reddens and swells, she lies against a chosen bull and twists about, stretches up to look at him or slides across his back as if mounting. Then he'll do a little barking, rub his whiskers along her body, and nip at her; she'll arch her back upward and spread her hind flippers. Sometimes their sex lasts a few minutes, sometimes an hour. And, like a male otter, he'll mount and dismount, fall asleep for a while, then get back to work. And when she's had enough, she'll rise up, bite him hard, and pull free, waddle away while he thrusts at the air.

The squall passed as the sun set, and the cove quickly grew dark. Willie and I came in together, pulled off our suits down along the water; waves washing almost to our feet, sky suddenly magenta and purple with huge blocks of cloud flat and black along the horizon. The sweetness of tiny yellow flowers fell pungent from the cliff, and I mentioned what a beautiful life this seemed to be, how much I'd hate to have to leave it. Willie knew just what I meant, said he'd been working all his life to hold on to this kind of freedom. Steve was last out of the water right at nightfall, still somewhat forlorn, and Willie remembered to ask if it was Steve's half-blind dog we'd found in the highway. It was, and Steve went a little pale when he heard where she'd been, thanked us a few too many times, said he just didn't want to lose her right now, that was all.

9

When Krakatoa erupted in 1883 in Indonesia, creating a blast heard three thousand miles away in Madagascar, a cataclysmic wave—a tsunami—ranging from 60 to 120 feet high, destroyed hundreds of towns and killed over 36,000 people. Seismic, benthic disturbances can do the same: in 1960 an 8.5 earthquake in Chile generated a tsunami that crossed the Pacific and leveled the city of Hilo in Hawaii. Then, of course, there are rogue waves, the occasional out-of-scale monsters formed by converging swells, the kind that are supposed to keep you from walking out exposed rock spits on otherwise flat days. Like the 112-footer encountered February 7, 1933, by the USS *Ramapo* in the North Pacific; a sailor on the bow apparently had the sangfroid to measure the wave's height by triangulating off a high point at the ship's middle. But as delicious as such tales are, the surfer lives around and for more mundane phenomena, wind waves and even tides, which are themselves waves half the circumference of the earth and half a day apart. The high tide, then, is a global crest, while the low is a global trough. And one rides the decaying pulses of far-off storms: solar heat and global winds create high and low pressure systems, areas of storm and areas of calm; a ridge over Oregon, a trough off Anchorage. Wind from the warmer high fills in the colder low and in transit makes a "fetch" over a stretch of sea, which makes waves: wind friction first ripples the water, then, pushing on the ripples, makes chop. Pushing on the chop makes a constant sea, which leaves the storm and fetch and rolls across open ocean, consolidating, compressing, combining into cleaner lines of swell, trains of waves. And in trains, the foremost wave constantly yields to the ones behind, and new ones appear in the back: a cycling through of shapes to produce a macro ripple, a revolving chunk of sine curve.

So the swell that rolls into harbor, so clean and so beyond storm, has traveled calm water for hundreds, even thousands of miles. When the pulse hits shallow water it slows and bends to the shape of the shoaling bottom; wave energy deflects off the bottom at an angle, steepening until breaking. One floats, then, waiting for a pulse from the sun, just so processed: the shape of the wave ridden is an expression of that faraway storm, of the shape of the seafloor over which one floats, of the precise direction from which a swell hits the seafloor, and of local winds. Onshore wind against the backs of the waves breaks them too soon; offshore into their faces holds them up beautifully steep and fast. And that ocean floor, rarely seen but intimately known: the shape and foam of breaking waves stain a white map of the bottom in liquid relief and motion. A surfer gets to know the benthic topography through its expression in the wave, through holes into which the wave vanishes and shelves over which it stands up. In fact, over the past few weeks, the rains had brought a near-constant audience to the far end of the cliff by my house: the overlook at the mouth of the San Lorenzo River. Every evening, guys gathered by the wooden rail to watch tons upon tons of silt flowing into the bay, sloshing through opaque brown breakers. Pulling their hats low in the downpour, they stood around chatting, speculating on whether this could be the year everyone's been waiting for, the year when the river-mouth sandbar finally regained the shape it had in the legendary winter of 1983. A year when similar, very wet "Pineapple Express" Pacific storms drew enough mud and sand out of the mountains in just the right formation to make a flawless tubular wave break for nearly a hundred yards. It hadn't come close since, but every year—especially in a wet year, like this one—there was hope.

And still, a certain *something* one wonders about in the wave, some hint of the "source," some fundamental means of energy transfer suggesting the essentially *energetic* nature of matter. So, call up an old-friend-cum-physicist:

"Our data says we've done it," the physicist pronounced, when I asked about his thesis experiment.

Done what?

"Built a clock that will count backwards if time reverses in the universe." He sounded dismayed, irritated. "And our data says we've done it."

Reversed time, or built the clock?

"The clock, but it can't be true, because if it is, I win the Nobel Prize."

I pictured his earnest blue eyes and sculpted, boyish face, tortoiseshell glasses. Then changed the subject, asked the big question: What the hell *are* waves, anyway?

He thought for a moment—an awkward silence in the delayed relay between Munich and California—then said, "Waves of radiation or light or sound—it's all elongated sinusoidal oscillations. You really want to get into this? Get a pen. Frequency's the distance between peaks; the peak's the sine and the trough's the cosine; think of amplitude as the wave height, which is basically the vertical distance from trough to crest, and wavelength as the horizontal distance from trough to crest, and the period's the time it takes a crest to travel a wavelength. So, when you're sitting out there, a wave moves toward you but the water doesn't: you probably move in a pretty circular orbit when that wave passes under you."

Energy, though?

"Certainly. Same as sound waves," he said, " 'cause energy's energy. And, uhh . . . I think there's about four hundred joules of energy in a cc of water at room temperature, so . . . that means one quantum for a water wave's about . . ." He stopped talking for a moment, and I heard tapping noises. "Zero point, oh, about thirty-three zeros and six joules. But a wave would have a lot of quanta. Joules per second is power, right? As in watts in your light bulb? So waves have power."

Indeed. I'm somewhat mealy-minded at things quantitative; in fact, the physicist had always embarrassed me in such discussions, made me cling to my belief in the great variety of human intelligence.

"Anyway," he said, "you got to understand some things about the water molecule—it's unbelievably hard, and hates to bend or stretch. So picture water like this. Get a pen." He talked me through a little sketch, mark at a time:

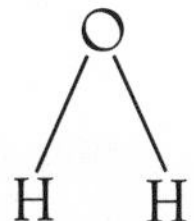

"And the bond's really strong," he said, "so water molecules like to endlessly stack on top of each other—sort of full-on group sex for most of the ocean. These stacks move in two ways: first, as a collective, and second, individually. In other words, the molecules can either bump into each other, or just vibrate alone." He coughed into the line, complained about the lousy weather in northern Europe. "So the ocean's frozen," he said, "rock-hard and nothing you'd call a wave. You hit it with a hammer and it rings a bit, right? So there's some sounds ice supports, basically really high wave frequencies. But melt it into a liquid, and the molecule bonds get looser. So now they're farther apart and take longer to bang into each other, giving you a lower resonant frequency—big, full-on waves. So what you're surfing," he said, suddenly changing tone, "is a giant collective undulation of stacked water molecules . . . Is that what you wanted to know?"

I supposed it was, and we chatted a little longer about the North America Wall, a gargantuan, five-day rock climb he'd done the month before on Yosemite's El Capitan. His hands had yet to heal, he said, still couldn't quite make a fist. He rambled a bit about his growing anxiety that he wasn't a true physics genius after all; they had usually peaked by his age, he said, solved some profound problem or redefined certain terms. A call came from an engaged friend of mine, inviting me to a wedding shower up in the city, and then I stepped outside. To corroborate the physicist's interpretation, I strolled down to the beach for a look: our walk in the park, our local copse or lane. It was a path I followed nightly now as well, even found a few familiar faces. Looked forward to the upcoming Christmas parade in the yacht harbor, in which sailboats motored along the docks at night, decked out in colored lights and electrified Santas and Nativity scenes. People with dogs, brooders, barefoot waders, and stumbling, inseparable couples. The sun setting a deep orange behind the west side of town. Above black silhouettes of eucalyptus and palm, a rich flaming band gave way to tropical purple, then to cobalt in the night behind. The orderly west swell of the last few days had faded to a murmuring jibberish, a pointless mumbling. One often hears surfers talk of waves in these terms, particularly on days when the bands are broken up and the interval too short, days when the sea resembles so much sloshing water rather than a field of rolling energy. "It's all confused," a guy will say, by way of visual description. I once even heard myself tell Willie of the water before us, without a trace of irony, "Dude, it's making *no* sense." I loved the implication that, at times of clean swell, the sea actually did make sense, as if it had some message to communicate, some language to speak. And at times of truly remarkable surf, when all the swell and wind vectors coincide with precisely the right tide to make your home break charge with life, it's as though the friend you've tolerated through weeks or months of doggerel has finally learned to sing the very pulse of the world. As if a speech normally hard to decipher, somehow *inarticulate*, has suddenly been uttered not just well, but in a language unmistakably meant for you; chaos reduced, at last, to a single idea. So when Vince rode his bike to the cliff each morning to calculate the day's optimal conflation of elements, he was, in a sense, looking for that moment when the world would intone just what he—and I—most wanted to hear.

Of course, different moments will sing different songs: stately and warlike Wagner during grand northwesters or, when the light breaks through storm clouds and a south swell catches the point perfectly square, the wit and mystical clarity of a Wallace Stevens lyric. (The evidence then for a divine hand seems awfully good.) I'd had a similar feeling once on the final headwall of a long route on El Capitan; we turned the lip of a big roof to see several hundred feet of polished, overhanging granite. Splitting the middle of that otherwise unclimbable expanse was a single perfect crack. The world then seemed to have a humane design; or, to take the other tack, my own relationship with the world seemed finally clear enough to recognize nature's capacity for precise expression. Waves do, after all, have a staggering complexity. Skinny had teased that I wouldn't be a real surfer until I bought myself a weather radio, and since I have quite a hang-up with authenticity, I'd scrambled out and bought one. Kept it on low volume at all times. As we all know, too much information can be a bad thing. The way nonstop TV coverage of a war or murder trial can tyrannize a person, so did these hourly wind updates tyrannize me, three hourly buoy reports complete with interval. This last figure, the average time elapsing between the passage of distinct wave peaks beneath the buoy, becomes in many ways the primary obsession: a nine-foot swell with a nine-second interval might register at the beach as only a feeble two or three feet; a nine-foot swell with a nineteen-second interval might register as nine feet and very powerful. So, whenever sitting there reading like a good boy, I occasionally heard a jump in average wave height or a lengthening of interval—hints of new swell—productivity plummeted. My quasi girlfriend had begun to find all this talk painfully tedious as she suffered through much of it on the phone, the unfortunate fabric of a long-distance relationship. She was quite alive to the birds and otters, even started keeping an Audubon bird book in her Toyota Celica in a sweet gesture of solidarity with me. But waves? Categorically uninteresting to her, although she'd even bought me a beautiful coffee-table book called *The Book of Waves* that Christmas. She just found them inert somehow. Not alive. About as interesting as rocks. Gendered concerns? Maybe.

A painter on disability who lived down the street had her evening Scotch on a concrete bench as I walked past; six feet and lanky, with an attractive, angular face. A woman I never got to know well, but with whom I exchanged regular, wearily complex smiles. The surly man with a big red beard sat on his usual bench and read; never with a friend or lover, just a book and a bag of walnuts. He also appeared every morning before dawn to, as he put it, "read the paper and watch the fishing boats head out." I'd noticed the next day that while he certainly read the paper, he always chose the one bench that did not allow a view of the departing boats. Two paddleboarders were out near the pier, but by and large swimmers held fast to the *Pequod*, stayed by the sand. At the southern end of the beach, a sandbar threw up a wedging collective undulation; four skimboarders in short-sleeved wetsuits held their boards, watching, not looking at one another, not talking. Then one trotted toward the water, finless plywood board held to one side and forward. He turned once, adjusted, then sprinted. At the inch-deep film of lingering water, he dropped the board, danced on, and skimmed into the muddy green face. He banked against it, ducked under its lip, and shot toward the beach, tubed. One second of glory before getting body-slammed. The other three guys stared away, bored.

A schooner sailed slowly past, visitor from the past surrounded by gawking modern sailboats; I tried to conjure Juan Cabrillo, George Vancouver, or Sir Francis Drake, wanted to imagine my beach precontact, but it wasn't here; only an Army Corps of Engineers harbor jetty had stopped up enough littoral drift to fill it in. To the west, one could see Lighthouse Point jutting into the bay and the great surf break at Steamer Lane. Mostly for this view, a procession of men passed here daily, parked their pickups on the way to work, sat a moment with the motor running. A few drove big Ford works trucks, clearly the general contractors; most drove the standard-issue surfer vehicle, the Japanese light pickup with fiberglass camper shell, four-wheel-drive only for those with Baja ambitions. They watched the Lane for swell, the outer bay waters for wind. A few came every day at lunch, rolled down a window and ate their sandwiches quietly—the ocean holding down a part of their lives, maintaining a self always renewing.

The lighthouse beacon turned pointlessly, and rills washed along the pilings of the tawdry pier just north, only occasionally thumping, never booming. The three-quarter moon hung as a flattened circle over a dusty Salinas sky to the southeast, and the Monterey ring of lights appeared due south, scribing the other side of the bay into the evening. A white sailboat drifted in the offshore, land-scented breeze and a big fishing boat sat near the pier. Earth and dry-grass smells, making the ocean seem less oppressively wild, more contained. Swimmers in no hurry to get out—a late trace of Indian summer without the cruel contrasts of high summer, without cold morning fog or blistering noon heat. I sat on the bench in a warm, gentle breeze with no impending storm, no unnerving drought or brooding fog: just a lovely evening in a lovely place. A silhouette dog chased a stick against anodized blue water scintillating with ambient crimson; a wave lifted dark over the sand, its back blocking out the dusk, and in the moment before collapsing—a pause like the death between breaths, the muteness between words—shot a streak of rising moonlight along its black face.

Later, sea lions barking under the pier and night fully come, the breeze reversed, blew cool off the Pacific and brought marine smells through my open window. I read once about a woman who closed her seaward windows at night to keep out the lost souls that wander the ocean's spaces.

10

Nobody understands. At that wedding shower for one of my oldest friends, I sat down with a big lunch at a lace-covered card table in an elegant Oakland Hills home. For some reason, surfing is *funny*. If you answered the "What have you been doing these days?" questions with "Training for a marathon" or "playing a lot of basketball," would anyone giggle? Would anyone act like you'd just said you'd been reenacting your childhood? Well, try it with surfing sometime, and you'll be surprised. The groom, for example, wanted to know just *exactly* how often I surfed.

"Oh," I said, pushing my potato salad around my maritime-patterned plate, "a lot." Relieved at not being the showered one, but also looking around the room, calculating my relative desirability as a mate with very poor results: no finance, no romance. I'd actually been a little stunned upon arrival; after rattling in the truck up a blustery late-fall coastline of sweeping white thunderheads and misting rows of surf booming through rocky coves, I'd pulled up to a vision almost as startling as the first wrinkles one finds in the mirror. When you're in school, you live more or less the same life as your peers: maybe they go out to sushi a little more frequently, or have surprising plastic freedom at Benetton, but you're all students. Living in student digs, doing homework, drinking cheap beer. But the longer you're out of college, the more pronounced become material differences, especially when people start getting married. Stopping my truck, I ran into one of my oldest friends in a smashing Italian suit, stepping out of a spanking new black BMW sedan. He didn't see me at first, and I felt as though watching the life-that-might-have-been on Candid Camera.

"You surf a lot," the groom said, mocking my drawl. "A lot. What's that supposed to mean?"

"Who's doing your catering?" I suddenly wanted to know. The theme appeared to be Americana, with a twist: gourmet New Mexico chicken/turkey "bird" dogs, oregano-spiced turkey burgers, sweet-potato home fries. Red-white-and-blue napkins and tablecloths. Parents milled about the kitchen and outside deck, mostly lawyers and doctors, some perhaps wistful about the glow of optimism at the "kids' " table where we all sat, some no doubt thankful to have those illusions well behind them. Early American antiques and replicas—a varnished old ice chest painted with faded Stars and Stripes, an American Eagle–framed mirror—gave the room that comforting combination of wholesome patriotism and burnished elegance. Like the stateroom of a nineteenth-century patrician ship's captain.

"Don't weasel," the groom insisted with a smile. Absolutely made for family life and already a district attorney, he had a knack for cross-examination: "More than once a week?"

"Sharon," I said to his beautiful and ironic fiancée, "you actually going to wear your mother's wedding dress?" I'd heard all about her embarrassment at the ten-foot train.

"More than once a day?" the groom demanded, hot on the trail now.

Much as the bride appeared to like me, to even approve of my life, she wasn't going to help me. "Well . . . Hey, Orin," I said to another guest, an ex-collegiate swimmer just returned from an investment banking training program on Wall Street, a handsome, friendly guy without quite enough mean bones in his body, "how's being back from New York? You getting some sunshine?"

"You actually go surfing more than once a day," the groom announced, nodding with astonishment. He put down his well-appointed sausage sandwich (cilantro, roasted bell peppers, honey mustard, grilled onions), wiped his mouth with a napkin, and said, "That's unbelievable!"

"Loving it," said Orin, the swimmer. "In fact, I'd love to . . ."

"Hold on, Orin," the groom demanded. "I'm not through with this bastard. You ever go out more than *twice* a day?"

Like I said, nobody understands. Surfing's a full-time job, and always has been. A writer in the 1896 *Hawaiian Annual* writes of Hawaiian surfers what any local could tell you today, that "necessary work for the maintenance of the family, such as farming, fishing, mat and tapa making, and such other household duties required of them and needing attention . . . was often neglected for the prosecution of the sport." And if Hawaiian petroglyphs are any indication, this terrible pattern had long, illustrious standing. Hawaiian historian Kepelino Keauokalani records that "expert surfers going upland to farm, if part way up . . . look back and see the rollers combing the beach, will leave work . . . hurrying away home they will pick up the board and go. All thought of work is left. The wife may go hungry, the children, the whole family, but the head of the house does not care. He is all for sport, that is his food. All day there is nothing but surfing." My decreasingly committed girlfriend, Susan, certainly saw it this way. In his 1847 *Residence of Twenty-one Years in the Sandwich Islands*—"an account of the efforts to raise [the Hawaiians] from their degradation and barbarism and convert them from their idols, their cruel superstitions, and their unbridled lusts"—American missionary Hiram Bingham explains the decline of Hawaiian surfing in similar terms: "the adoption of our costume, greatly diminishes their practice of . . . sporting in the surf, for it is less convenient to wear it in the water than the native girdle, and less decorous and safe to lay it entirely off on every occasion they find for a plunge or swim or surf-board race." Truly Edenic—putting on clothes, they discover shame; discovering shame, they stop surfing.

"Less time, moreover," Bingham continues, "is found for amusement by those who earn or make cloth-garments for themselves like the more civilized nations." So, with clothing as civilization and honest labor the way to get it, the surfer stops hanging out at the beach, gets dressed, and goes to work—at least in theory. So long ago, and yet so familiar. Besides, the islander now has a responsibility to colonial capitalism. "Indeed," Bingham explains, "the purchase of foreign vessels . . . required attention to the collecting and delivering of 450,000 pounds of sandal-wood, which those who were waiting for it might naturally suppose would, for a time, supersede their amusements." Naturally—with a delivery schedule to meet, Kanaka ain't got time. School, another distraction to the serious surfer, also contributes: "The heathen sports of the nation nearly disappeared," Bingham explains, with the advent of "elementary instruction in reading, writing, morals, religion, arithmetic, geography, sacred song, and sacred history." One has to wonder what is distinctly "heathen" about surfing, for certainly there *is* something un-Christian, nonlinear, non-Western, even, about the sport. The lack of a goal, perhaps? Of quantifiable achievement? One must also, I think, admire the hubris of Bingham's causal chain—like linking the rounding up of the Lakota Sioux to the contemporaneous formation of the first professional baseball leagues.

A few days after the wedding shower, Orin the swimmer drove down from San Francisco to try surfing with me, take the waters.

After three years amassing a starter fortune, he was back out west, looking for roots, authenticity—wanted to pick up either surfing or martial arts. A close mutual friend had died the previous fall of a sudden heart attack, and Orin had given up an enormous salary and a place in an MBA program to take over the friend's nonprofit organization, using corporate finance techniques to actually help people. And his making the drive down counted as a gesture of friendship with me: he enthused at great length about the serenity of my life, how all I did was write and surf. I usually felt uncomfortable with praise for a life the speaker would never remotely consider—life choices imply values that chitchat sometimes obscures—but Orin just had the grace and good humor to be enthusiastic about other people's lives in a way that made you feel good about your own. He also meticulously, thankfully avoided unfortunate comparisons with his own great success.

We walked out the road together and found it muddied and slippery from the heavy rains. The remaining brussels sprouts clustered thick like a miniature jungle in rows and rows of muted sage green. The harvested field was now black and wet under the cloud-broken sky. The roadside hemlock had begun to mold from the rain, and the season's first shoots of new grass and thistle had appeared, a thrusting little chi fest of the sun that follows rain. We slid down the eroding trail, then changed on the rock below the cliff. Soon we were among big, disorganized peaks still confused from the storm. Usually, a beginner in cold water will last between thirty and forty minutes, but Orin had been such a powerful swimmer in high school and college that he stayed with me for hours with no fatigue—endlessly smiling and delighted as he got clobbered by wave after wave, out of his mind with joy when he actually rode one to the beach. Vince paddled out alone just as Orin and I agreed to head in; he smiled a mirthless greeting that revealed his irritation with me. I'd brought an utterly unskilled outsider into his kitchen; and as antisocial as this seems, I'd come to understand his feelings. Once a break becomes widely known, it will never again retreat into obscurity; indiscretion in conversation at night can mean the difference between a lovely morning with your friends and a tense struggle in a crowd for the rest of the season.

Vince did warm up to Orin soon enough, largely because Orin didn't know enough about the surfer code of cool to be anything other than his jovial, outgoing self. But even as they chatted between waves I could hear a tone of reserve in Vince's voice; he seemed to feel that Orin's delight was much like the delight one expresses in a foreign country, mistaking one's attraction to the simple lives of the locals for true sympathy of spirit with them. And perhaps Vince was right, but, like I said, Orin also meant well, and at least he'd made the drive down here on a weekday to spend some time; he also had the courtesy and openness to make conversation with Vince, and thus acknowledge Vince's status as landlord.

Drying off in a patch of dead grass under the trees, Orin called First Boston in Manhattan on his cellular phone to ask about a potential investor. His diction changed easily to that of a professional money manager; as he made his pitch, he watched Vince intently, Vince the grown-up, still in the water, alone, on a remote beach, late on a Monday morning. The whole world at work while this educated, middle-class adult walked the nose for a clean five, cut back into the foam, launched himself into the air as Orin's little phone satellite-linked Orin to the distant office of a distant analyst. Apparently satisfied with the call, Orin put the phone back in his pocket and started cogitating: brow knit, hands clenching—in a moment of transition himself, considering the alternatives—he kept looking back at Vince, alone and apparently unconcerned about the impending lack of audience.

"Does he . . . work?" Orin asked. Orin's eye then swept out to sea, up to the just-greening hills, and back; at a break and a sport Vince had been studying for thirty years, his whole professional and personal life organized around its demands. Promotions missed, tenure never a possibility, no pension or job security. Most of every day's best energy burned in the water. "I can't believe nobody's figured out how to tax this," Orin said with delight. "I mean . . . it's free!"

11

Magazines tell a lot about a person: two months into a life of water-based anonymity, having not been awake past ten o'clock more than once, nor asleep past six more than two or three times, and being too self-conscious to go on-line in search of virtual friends, I had unwittingly sought company via the U.S. Postal Service: *Outside*, a fun smorgasboard of adrenaline-oriented play; *Sierra*, a by-product of my Sierra Club membership, gleaned in a moment of guilt-driven good intention when an attractive canvasser appeared at my door; *Surfing*, apparently targeted at the fourteen-to-sixteen-year-old set, but packed with great photographs, good for about two solo lunch sittings and a week or two of bathroom duty; *Surfer*, for the eighteen-to-twenty crowd, but actually containing a little text, a highlight of my month; *The Surfer's Journal*, at nine bucks an issue, a pricey subscription, but its quarterly serving of long, thoughtful surf-nostalgia articles took care of almost a week of solo dinner sittings, while its magnificent photography merited collection status; *Climbing*, just to remind me of who I'd been, of a former set of ambitions; *Rolling Stone*, as a stand-in for an actual social life; and, lastly, *The New Yorker*, gift of Mom and Dad after it had published a beautifully written two-part article on surfing at San Francisco's Ocean Beach—not quite assiduous enough in their general coverage of the sport, but interesting nonetheless.

The magazines appeared weekly in our rusted metal mailbox, right there on the porch where rotted two fabulous old upholstered chairs, recliners such as would've made perfect thrones in the backyard opera of a ten-year-old. I think the magazines suggested a profligacy of mind to my housemates, particularly the Reef Brazil sandal ads that appeared in all the surf mags: on the first or second page of every issue stood some bronzed islander girl with a thong bikini pulled taut. The view, of course, was the one the reader presumably found most familiar: the furtive, undetected glance from behind. I'd resisted the temptation to take *Longboarder's Journal*, *Longboarding*, and *Australian Surfing Life*, for fear of entirely losing identity in a swirling collage of wave-action centerfold posters pinned to my bathroom walls, of daily surf-shop visits to fondle boards and watch their never-ending video screenings. The primary haunt for the latter had become Pacific Wave Surf & Snow, a shop new enough to treat weird older guys like me with respect. I'd stopped shaving regularly, gotten less bookish eyeglass frames, and had even taken to wearing flip-flop sandals and dark-colored sweatshirts with the hood pulled low indoors. I never entirely achieved the look, but the guys at Pacific Wave seemed not to mind the hours I spent on their sales floor, gazing at their video monitors, spending no money as I stood hypnotized, envious of the effortless grace of L.A. teenagers on impossible, corporate-financed South Seas surfaris.

And lousy weather and high winds had increasingly rendered the Point useless, forced a fellow to participate in the human drama and surf the more crowded breaks in town. When the swell got too wild for the open coast of the Point, you just had to come in to market, where the arc of the bay and wall of the Santa Cruz

Mountains protected reefs from fierce northerly winds. No place on earth feels more deliciously like the civic fray of a surf town than Steamer Lane, a series of breaks running alongside a stretch of cliff in the heart of Santa Cruz. A fabulous public arena and promenade along which one can sit on benches with lunch on a warm day or coffee on a cold one, face south across the adamantine blue of the bay, and look right down on big surf expertly ridden, a whole human economy of hustle, showmanship, and shared municipal pleasure. Beaming men and women walk dripping on the sidewalk, filled with both the pleasure of physical well-being and the pride of membership, like wearing a mountaineer's getup in Chamonix. Clearly one is part of the main event: "Yes, in fact, I *am* in the band."

And if Richard Henry Dana's Hawaiian friends never got around to surfing in San Diego in the 1830s, then in all likelihood the Hawaiian princes David, Cupid, and Edward Kawananakoa were the first to do it on the mainland, at the Seabright beach by my house. Attending a San Mateo school in the 1880s, they saw the gently peeling waves at the mouth of the San Lorenzo River and decided to ride them: bought redwood planks at a local lumber mill, had them properly planed, and gave Santa Cruz what became one of its defining features. Duke Kahanamoku himself, the worldwide ambassador of surfing and Olympic Gold Medal swimmer who was eventually recruited by Hollywood as a handsome, manly Polynesian who could pass for all manner of swarthy types, from Indian chiefs to Arabs, appeared for water carnivals at the Santa Cruz beach boardwalk in the 1930s. The Santa Cruz Surf Museum holds black-and-white photographs of the old surf clubhouse—a little white shack by the beach—with a few smiling boys in front, healthy and simple, dapper. Back in the 1950s when you made your eleven-foot, one-hundred-pound redwood board in wood shop. Fred Van Dyke remembers those good old days of camping in cars at Steamer Lane (by the lighthouse) and Pleasure Point, in caves by the river mouth. "It was a slow life on that clean beach," he recalls, "with the smell of baitfish skipping on the surface and fog hanging outside; the water not as choppy as Steamer Lane. It was our northern Malibu." And no wetsuits: a fifteen-cent wool shirt from Goodwill and paddling on your knees got you about thirty minutes of water time before you had to thaw your hypothermic body at a driftwood bonfire. Van Dyke remembers board-surfing a wave as a friend bodysurfed it; a chinook salmon leapt out in front and a sea lion rode behind. He even recalls befriending a seal those days alone in the water, an aquatic familiar that returned his board when it got away.

One bright blue autumn afternoon, onshore winds slopped up the Point on their way down the coast but wrapped around the bay mouth, eddied up against the Santa Cruz Mountains, and turned offshore at the lighthouse, blowing the surf clean and straight. Sixty surfers out, bicyclists in the autumn sunshine, a local roller skater doing his daily dance on old, two-axle skates; the archetypal Golden Age Surfer stood in bronze in a flower garden, a man of medium build with a crew cut and well-defined muscles, wearing shorts (!) and holding a huge longboard in the old manner: propped upright against his back, held from behind with both hands. Around his neck hung a fresh lei of flowers, and a nearby bench was dedicated "In Memory of All Surfers Who Have Caught Their Last Wave." (The cities of Santa Cruz and Huntington Beach went to court recently over the right to the appellation "Surf City.") I pulled on my wetsuit as a stream of dripping surfers marched by—rides so long, inbound current so strong, a hike along the cliff was the only sensible way back out. And no wilderness about it; at the bottom of the stairs a grizzled dope smoker in mirrored shades offered free "attitude adjustments." Big "A-frames" broke far outside while speed walls reeled along the cliff; I loitered at the latter, duck-diving and waiting until I caught a long one and got lost playing its pulse, its suck and throw. A lip started to throw out ahead—the part you slam, the shredee—and I unweighted across its breaking back: a wonderful moment of weightlessness before landing with the foam.

Back outside: overpopulation, limited resources, no eye contact, paddling with back arched to indicate poise, aggression—the worst thing you can do is lie limp across your board, suggesting improper adaptation and resolve. So you keep your head up in the crowd, stroke forcefully in what is a very cultured space: rigid traffic rules to obey, a very clear code for claiming waves. But then I caught a wave fair and square and none other than Apollo dropped in front of me, clearly violating the traffic rules. He suddenly seemed so small, so adolescent, that I let him twitch and thrash his way along until I could give him a gentle shove out the back of the wave. His face locked up with fury as I passed by, and he tried to hit my board with his; failing that, he screamed something about how he should shoot his board at my head. When I'd ridden the wave out and paddled back, I found myself in perfect position to return the favor Apollo had done me, and did.

"What are you doing?" he screeched, as I dropped in front of him.

"Burning you," I said with a smile, "like you burned me." Fading back to the curl, I forced him into the white water, thus out of the wave. Afterwards, I paddled up to him, asked what he had expected.

"You don't know what you're doing," he said with great distaste. Several of his friends had turned to watch.

"But," I said, "honestly. You know the rules, right, you little shit? You dropped in on me, you saw me there, and you never pulled out, did you?" He giggled nervously at my anger, and then I lost control, gave him my whole I-could-have-an-Uzi scenario at full volume before working my way through a reminder of the longboarder's lesson and a guilt-inducing, I'm-mostly-disappointed-with-you harangue. When I was done, Apollo looked more like a cowed child than a real adversary, and I started to feel like a cad. Shamefaced and trying to keep smiling, the little punk turned to a bearded man floating next to me. "Hey, Dad," he said quietly, "you want to just get one more and then go in?" Interesting: Dad was a perfectly strong surfer who couldn't have been vaguely intimidated by me, but he hadn't said a word through all that abuse. Must have felt the little bastard deserved it.

But then, even as I felt righteous, a kayaker snuck behind me on a great wave and I cracked, took off in front of *him*, violating the same rule Apollo had. We dodged and feinted up and down the wave face until he drove into the curl and fell behind. Later, the spurned one paddled his star-speckled boat over and, hot-faced and knowing he couldn't win, said, "Pull another stunt like that and I'll run your ass over."

Heavy. "Take your cheap fucking toy somewhere else," I found myself saying, "or learn how to surf." The only escape was up the stairs, among strollers and joggers, and out to the end of the Point. The antisocial misfit eschews human companionship, so I slipped down the worn natural steps, tossed the board in, and leapt after it. A loon popped up after ducking a wave and three sea lions stuck out their heads to take a gander—they had a noisy little colony on an offshore rock. A 180-degree rainbow touched down in the water, connecting the misty green hills to the sparkling white pier, and gilded thunderheads passed over: rain, then clearing, then downpour, then sunshine. And then, as I breathed deeply and replayed my last conversation, I realized I had become what I most despised. So I floated and watched awhile, gazed at the tight pack of locals who knew the ins and outs of this reef so beautifully they made every launching aerial or gouging turn seem perfectly instinctive, fluid. There were also a few older longboarders who knew the wave well enough to be on their feet before it broke, and a couple of older shortboarders appeared to be aging heavies, their status as alpha males unchallenged. Add the rest of the hundred or so humans now in the water and the Lane became a joint-expression session for an entire town: hippies with saltwater dreadlocks, bleached Nazis still lost in the late 1980s, students trying to fit in without disrespecting the indigenous peoples.

"Can I tell you a story?" asked a red-nosed guy in a white-and-blue wetsuit, floating nearby.

"Of course," I said.

"Low tide yesterday, I'm out here with a couple guys, and this otter's floating by on his back and he's got this beer can and he's holding it like he's drinking. So I say, 'Hey, I wonder what kind of beer he's drinking.' Guy next to me goes, 'Why ask why?' Good, huh? Huh?"

Happily, before I had to respond, a wave lumbered in: carving and soaring in the breeze, clear to the inner cove. And just as I flopped off my board, I saw him: the kayaker, the only human whose forgiveness could cleanse my sins. As I paddled toward him, his jaw set and his eye flitted back and forth from the horizon to me. Preparing for war.

"Look," I said, sitting up. "I obviously need to see a psychiatrist. I was a complete asshole to you back there, and I'm really sorry about it."

The kayaker was so surprised, it took him a moment to get my meaning; but when he did, he smiled broadly (and has ever after greeted me warmly when our paths have crossed). Walking belaboredly up the concrete steps, feeling the world too much with me and quite ready for intermission, I heard a tiny towhead ask in his little falsetto if the waves were any good. "Bitchin'," I told him, and he marched past saying, "Better be! I rode my bike all the way across town!"

I saw Vince on the sidewalk, by the Statue of the Unknown Surfer, wearing clean, faded blue jeans, a bright white T-shirt, sandals, and a weathered bill cap. He sat on his rusty, balloon-tired one-speed bike, leaning against the cliff railing, at once hawklike and boyish—as if chasing perfection for so long, he'd grown into a pleasantly self-satisfied hedonism, identified the things worth getting, and gotten them. "Fun out there?" he asked.

"Yeah, I got a few."

"Really? I didn't see that."

"Oh, well, yeah. A while ago. Missed you yesterday at the Point."

"Sucked, didn't it?"

"Yeah," I said, panting and dripping, lamenting a three-hour quest all over the county. "Ended up in that piddling nada at the Point."

"I could have told you that from the cliff in our neighborhood. Landing was perfect," he added, always the guy who'd scored while you floundered. Then, watching the water, he laid it out: "Point's never good on a due north swell, and anyway, it's already lost all that sand on the reef."

Just what I'd seen but couldn't name: deeper water inside, making the wave vanish beneath me.

"You got that new board yet?" he asked.

I hadn't.

He grinned knowingly, then said, "Beautiful, huh?" He gazed wistfully at the scene before us, still on his bike, sandaled feet on the pedals.

I looked around, tried to see what he saw: nice-enough day,

awfully blue water and sky if you could forget about all the humans muddying it up, all the inevitable ugliness of competition for resources.

"Just so . . . so clean," he said, mesmerized by the waves going by and not even seeing the hordes riding them, a delighted connoisseur of a taste cultivated over a lifetime, as if in aestheticized appreciation of another man's wife. Thirty years later, the hometown gem still owned his heart. And from here on the cliff there *was* something different about the ocean today, if you ignored the crowds. Calm, shiny, unruffled waves glided through still water as unhurried arcs of energy. Nothing chaotic, nothing violent, just a green pulse of glass softly spilling into white. Surfers took off without struggle: stroked, stood up, flowed down the runway and participated in the orderly push of a benign sea. Enough for a man who, I had learned, had surfed hot Indonesian barrels and lived alone in the Canary Islands to see in a smallish day at an urban break a rare and serene grace—just the right point between high and low tides, a strong but not-too-big swell coming from just the right angle in the western Pacific, wind lightly offshore holding the waves up before they broke, almost no ambient chop. The moment was all the more precious for the knowledge that tomorrow, perhaps even in an hour, it would pass.

As my black wetsuit heated in the sun and I forgot about the profound trauma to my inner *wa*, I thought how, with the peeling wave as an ideal of perfection, the surfer's object of passion becomes the very essence of ephemerality—not a thing to be owned or a goal to be attained but rather a fleeting state to inhabit. So much more of my time, after all, passed in the dreaming and searching than in the actual riding of waves; so much more time spent driving the coast and floating between sets. Of a whole year of devotion, probably no more than a day was spent truly on my feet and surfing, so I couldn't view such a moment as this without an ardent, frustrated desire, a near-religious craving for wholeness. Unlike so many other passions: while one might, I suppose, wish for a bloom to remain in blossom, for a ripening grape to hang always on the vine—yearnings John Keats made his own, for fleeting beauty and youth, the understandably hopeless hope that we might freeze our world's better moments—the wave's plenitude is rather in the peeling of the petal, the very motion of the falling fruit.

12

Dark, hard rain on the highway as I passed a splattered skunk and a broken house cat. I'd just been in Berkeley for the weekend with Susan: a great loin roast with Zinfandel, a few rented movies, and the Sunday paper. Just because she didn't sentimentalize budget beach shacks in backwater towns, Susan's needs and desires were by no means crassly materialistic. She just wanted a good, quiet cohabitational relationship, maybe the occasional discussion of a mutual future. She even pretended not to mind when, that very morning—in spite of its being a rainy Sunday, and in spite of my having done none of the reading for class the following morning—I'd left her place early to drive down the coast. Just had to see the water in this wintry mood.

And now, a few miles north of Santa Cruz, a bird the size of a large turkey stood square in my headlights: a great blue heron looking calm, poised, and nearly invisible with its long, knob-kneed legs and broadly webbed feet. It peered curiously about Route 1 as rows of headlights approached from both directions—such a vision of hapless elegance. I honked and it spread its wings in the downpour, lifted heavily off the asphalt, and dragged a few times at the laden air. I pulled over to watch as it landed and walked slowly about a turnout where a dirt road ended. Alone in this pelting storm (the whole state flooding, Russian River taking out homes, San Lorenzo turning the whole bay brown, beaches washing away), it stepped in its awkward elegance to a muddy stream where water drained from scrub-willowed hills and ran along a dirt road, under an aluminum fence. The bird stood in that simulacrum of a lagoon and drew its neck back like a bowstring, then thrust into the half inch of water. It plucked and spit out a dirt clod as though it were a sand crab in a tidal flat (even I, sitting in my pickup with the heater on and wipers going, could see it was a clod).

And the next evening, herons again: storm passed and clouds high, windows open, reading before dinner, breeze billowing the curtains and the palm rustling too (I'd savaged that palm the Saturday before—do you know that palm wood cuts like butter? I went through the small shoots with six hatchet strokes each). The maple tree outside rippled with a fall blaze, like the one single tree I remembered from four years in upstate New York. Not that I didn't remember whole hillsides of them, but there was only one particular tree that I remembered just for itself. It was also a maple, standing wildly bright yellow, not a single leaf out of color, electrified on the edge of a shale gorge. So blatantly transitory, those New England colors, such an oblique study in the temporality of beauty. By contrast, the maple out here seemed only a reminder of such sweet misfortune, as if one might forget loss and change amid the cool, sunny clarity of a Mediterranean autumn.

A loud, irritated "Caw!" came down Atlantic Street while its denizens were off at work. "Caw!" in a croaking, throaty voice as two great blue herons loped upwind directly before my wide-open window. What a gift! Those nearly rectangular wings so out of scale with their slender necks and bodies, bodies that bent with each wingbeat like fish weaving through water. One of the birds held its neck straight, its head fully a foot and a half in front of its shoulders, its thin neck giving, bending between beating body and breathing beak—a slender, elegant soul riding a dinosaurian stem. The other bird's neck hooked back like a pelican's, perching that little chip of a head amid the body feathers like a Cessna cockpit on a 747. Their wings beat at about the pace of my morning's heartbeat—even and without the urgency of the hunt or the scamper of scavenging—as they strode over my ungroomed lawn and its smattering of found art, its beheaded female bronze whose stump of a neck coyly lowered to the fig tree.

When I stepped outside to watch, the herons were gone. But it was high time for my sunset stroll anyway. I sat out on a bench and watched a beach bonfire surrounded by a large family singing in Italian. The whole beach strewn with driftwood as an elderly Eastern European couple in drab clothing splashed in the muddy shore break, laughing and hugging. The man with the ponytail from up the street—an architect—stood at the rail nearby, staring. Tall, white-haired, and handsome, he came down twice daily, usually alone: once at dawn, once at dusk, keeping an eye, reminding himself of something. We'd chatted a few times before and I'd grown to like him; he tended to ramble in very Zen terms about painting and poetry, meditation and the virtues of the quiet life, all of which were high on my own list. With two kids grown and gone, he lived with his second wife in a tiny second-floor studio apartment by an empty lot of high grass and flowers. Gulls circling in the warmth, I asked about his wife, a Native American with whom he'd lived for twenty years. She was reading from her manuscript tonight, he told me, at a Sun Dance benefit at the Veterans Hall. "Not much work for architects these days," he said, "but Jesus, she's great: big New York publishing houses going nuts for a full-blooded woman telling her story." He mentioned something about most Native writing having been done by mixed-blood authors, how her work represented a real step forward. I'd seen him a few days before as well. At a neighborhood café in the late morning, he'd been drinking decaf and looking through want ads of papers from faraway places: *Chicago Sun-Times*, *Detroit Free Press*, *Seattle Times*.

Clear sky, winter's deep blue overhead and late summer's paler haze still along the horizon, soft offshore breeze lifting the beach break into green barrels; outer bay waters whitecapping, not yet a driven sea, just white flecks on blue. Everybody's front-yard flower gardens sparkling with calla lilies, irises, poppies, lupine, sweetly pungent alyssum. These beach-cottage neighborhoods, with their narrow lanes and sidewalks of dirt and grass, their unkempt yards and delightful little flower gardens, shingles and stained-glass windows, old cars and dog porches, had a very human feel, entirely at odds with the astronomical cost of local real estate.

With that white hair swept off his tan brow, the architect looked slender and strong; his jeans and sweater were sun-bleached and his skin was mottled and falling slightly, lids hanging over blue eyes. Something furtive about the way he wouldn't look right at me.

"And you?" I asked.

"Oh," he said, as if embarrassed, "just having a look at the beach."

"Lovely place to watch the water, huh?"

"Yep, yep," he agreed quickly, nodding, "always changing. Never quite the same, light and wind and all."

I told him there'd been a fat west swell this week, and he nodded heavily. "All comes from the sun," he said, shoving his hands in his pockets, rocking back on his heels, "cooling and heating the earth, of course." He looked out to sea, then glanced sideways at me. I *was* interested. "Solar energy, you know, causing different densities in the atmosphere." He modeled the globe with his hands, then elaborated: "So you get winds, and then you get friction on the water, and then—there you have it—waves. And they even get pulled by gravity across the earth, slowly diminishing. Out there on your board, you're riding sun, wind, gravity, and tectonic *and* littoral drift all at once."

Deep. I thought the guy was an architect.

We stood leaning against that rail for a moment, feeling the breeze and watching the parched grass wave.

"*And*," he said, "the sun's our only *income* of energy, so every wave's an expression of the very astral gift of life to the planet." Then he coughed and his tone changed as he told me he'd been doing water drawings lately, extrapolating various swell directions across a page to see what "sea" it produced—a lot of unemployed time in that sun-filled studio. He talked for a while by this patch of ice plant along someone's ivy-covered fence, using many hand gestures to show how these drawings had gone, how, Say you had a big swell from here, the wake of that boat, the wash of your surfboard rail, a faint swell from the other side of the globe, local wind, a little backwash . . . all making a local pattern and a local meaning. And the guy didn't even surf, just went swimming occasionally.

"But the main thing in my life now," he said, nodding with the practical confidence of one announcing a decision to buy mutual funds, "is the horizon."

The horizon. *Honestly?*

He looked out at the one in question: "Yeah," he said, nodding again, "that line lets you know you're living in space." The evening breeze had cleaned up a sharp, absolute border between dark water and pale sky.

"Right off the edge of the earth," he said, "the whole planet's curve right here in your daily life. Lets you know you're on a spaceship.

"Anyway," he said abruptly, turning to leave, "you don't just look at it for a while and say, 'Okay, I've got that one figured out.' "

13

Vince, on the other hand, *did* have it all figured out: "Riding fence," he said with pleasure as we drove north together for the first time, passing break after break. "Surveying the domain, right? Got to at least go out and have a look every day—working on the country-gentleman model: even if you don't come home with a pheasant for dinner, you had your walk in the woods." Touring our cult's shared religious sites, hashing out their nuances, and just generally packing the world into comfortable little boxes. Vince had a tidy Japanese truck with no dents, clean paint, and an immaculate interior, all quite a contrast to my beaten-up, slovenly, all-around mistreated version of the same vehicle. Tide book slotted neatly in the ash-free cigarette tray, even a paper clip holding it open to the current month, clean foam pads in the back for surfboard protection, no stickers, no mirror hangings, no tears in the upholstery: it was a clean set of wheels to match his ironed work shirt, shaven face, and white teeth.

I finally had my new board, after nearly a month: Jack had dropped it off the night before in a fit of good conscience. He seemed apologetic about more than just the tardiness, but to my eye the board looked glorious, not least because underneath the fiberglass, right next to the penciled design specs, were the words "Shaped for Dan." Vince didn't seem impressed, said he could tell how a board would work the second he held it in his hands: just thirty years of soaking up data, storing it in those fingertips. A board had to feel alive at first touch, or he'd have nothing to do with it. Another peculiarity: Vince talked, as did many, about some boards just "not working," and other similar boards being absolute magic. Given that the differences are too subtle for a nonsurfer to even notice, and that they have no moving parts, the idea that a board could just not work didn't quite sit with me. Figured the proof would be in the water.

Vince had picked me up just after dawn, and we'd already surveyed nearly thirty miles of beach south of Santa Cruz; hadn't found a single sandbar to his liking, and were now speeding toward Willie's place up on the coast.

"By the way," I said to Vince, as we approached the farm on which Willie lived, "what does Willie do for a living?" The question had been nagging somewhat: decent car, nice clothes, more good dentistry, no apparent obligations.

Vince actually laughed out loud at the question, as though he'd been wondering when I'd ask. "Unclear," he said, looking sideways at me and raising his eyebrows. A big trailer truck passed in the other direction, laden with crates of sprouts.

"You don't have any idea?" I got a twinge that Willie wouldn't appreciate this conversation if he could hear it. Vince had also mentioned that Willie might not like our barging in on him without a phone call, but since he screened all calls, it was hard to make plans on the fly.

"He claims to work on the farm up there," Vince said, "but I have never, in ten years, *ever* known him to miss a swell. And hey, travel? No problem. Six weeks in Chile last summer, Costa Rica this summer . . . You know he lived in Indo, don't you?"

"Where?"

Vince slowed to a stop as another car signaled to turn left across the highway. "Indonesia," Vince said. "This is the part I'm not totally clear on. He apparently dropped out of Harvard in the seventies, but other than that . . . *misterioso*." He turned right onto a dirt road and followed it for almost a mile up the hillside beneath dense oak trees; the road made several turns before opening onto a broad dirt lot full of rusting cars. I saw no house, and the two long, windowless brown buildings bordering the lot looked like boarded-up barracks or toolsheds. A once-yellow cultivator rusted near a chicken-wire cage full of household garbage; a few white T-shirts and a pink pair of women's underwear hung from a line. Behind, open fields gave an unbroken view across the hills, over the muted-green of the artichoke fields on the other side of the highway, and out to a broad expanse of glaring white sea. The whole place felt as if perched on some airy, flying plane of green-and-brown earth, a speck of land soaring among all that windswept water and sweeping sky, and away from town and the highway a palpable calm reigned in the silence. A big Labrador slept in the grass by a white Plymouth with no tires, and a silver-haired man with bright brown eyes and smooth, rosy skin smiled hello from a chair by one of the sheds—at peace in a small patch of sunshine. "World expert on basil," Vince said softly to me: one life devoted to play, another to pesto. Vince mentioned that the property belonged to the basil guy, and that Willie apparently paid no rent.

We left the truck near Willie's El Camino and walked under the shade of an oak tree to a door in a shed. Vince knocked lightly on the peeling plywood, and soon the door opened.

"Coño," Vince said with a smile.

"Yeah, now," Willie responded. He said that he was, in point of fact, more than delighted to pursue waves; had been just about to head out himself. He welcomed us inside while he went for his board and wetsuit, and what a revelation! Waxed cedar floors and

cabinets, a huge case of books, three classical guitars, and the entire west-facing wall a series of floor-to-ceiling windows—outside, beyond a weathered deck and a small garden crowded with culinary herbs and salad greens (squalor renovated to unpretentious splendor), the Pacific Ocean beamed its overwhelming calm into every square inch of Willie's domestic life. Willie's beautiful wife, Pascale, sat at a handmade dining table, drinking espresso and reading *The New York Times*. A warm blend of Old World femme fatale and good-humored New Age feminist, Pascale seemed at once irritated and amused by the mustering of the troops, tickled by a life associated with such adult dereliction.

"Four days off I have," she said in a mock-Brooklyn accent to Vincent, whom she clearly knew well. "Four days! Any mention of plans? Any, like, 'Gee, honey, why don't we get away together?' No way! It's just like"—here her voice took on a flawlessly modulated, unexaggerated surfer accent—" 'Sorry, can't say what the waves'll be doing.' " Then she turned back to her paper, muttering, "It's pathetic." Something wonderfully good-humored about the complaint, though, in spite of that element of seriousness present in every joke. I looked over the books while she and Vince talked: mostly American poetry and minority women novelists; a few stretching manuals and a book on women's health. Willie came back inside with his board and asked Pascale for a few bucks. Pascale pointed to her purse and grinned to herself as she read the sports section—turned out she had a thing for baseball—and she seemed to have been only playing the carping wife for Vince and me, as if perfectly conscious of all these little male independence fantasies, and comfortable tweaking them.

Crowded together in Vince's truck, we drove back down to the highway, then farther north, stopping at a series of watersheds; where each creek emptied into the sea, we climbed up berms or out to cliff edges, surveyed the water. None of the reefs were catching the swell quite right, so we kept pushing north, talking back and forth in an endless fiddling with variables: this spot's taking the swell bigger, but the tide's going to get too low soon, Point might be better in a little while, but the wind's only going to worsen, crowds'll probably show up pretty soon, could wait for the lower tide and try another spot, but what about the storm front coming down?

"Chummies?" Vince suggested, referring to a break in which a dive operator had begun dumping tons of chum—pig blood and animal parts—to attract great whites.

"Feeling chummy?" Willie asked.

"Could be perfect."

"No guarantees in this life, but, *hey now*. We're on the road, the road's a fine place to be, you boys are good company . . . Might behoove a fellow to have a look. But, of course, might behoove us to just get wet, too."

"Wetness," Vince responded. "The old hand-in-the-bush theory." Where Willie tended to advocate picking a spot and deciding to be happy with it, Vince always deferred to the greener grass that might be elsewhere. He also claimed an indisputable authority on every variable affecting nearly every break in the county, which made negotiation difficult. But after nearly an hour more of haggling and contributing to the greenhouse effect, we—*they*, really—agreed upon "Chums," much to my dismay. So we stopped where yet another creek emptied across a beach, scrambled among detritus from what must have been a spectacular wreck—a twisted car body, a crank shaft, a radiator—then walked out past white ranch buildings, knobcone and Monterey pine and a strip of chaparral hunted by a black-shouldered kite.

A band of clouds stretched from horizon to horizon with ribs forming a vaporous spinal cord; pulverized shells mixed with black pebbles gave a shimmer to the beach's crunching surface. Carnage, too: a big elephant seal with its bottom half bitten off and a bright red organ swelling out of the hole, flaps of muscle hanging pale pink and white. Two flippers lay against its side like mortified hands, and a gull stood serenely nearby, looking away from the object of interest—as those birds do—into the middle distance. Patient and unafraid, the gull let us pass by before plucking out the seal's eyes. A little farther along in the kind of daily excursus for which I'd begun to live, the wave almost a chimera to justify day after day of wandering obscure stretches of sand, analyzing the relationships of a reef's bottom contours to prevailing winds and various swell directions, we crossed yet another creek coming down from the mountains, spilling into a cobble of stones that had whorls like wood grain. And there, still more carnage: a decapitated otter, broken bones jutting through stiffened skin and the truncated spine sticking like a broken flag pole into the air. Great whites apparently didn't eat otters, just beheaded them. Two very large vultures attended the corpse, perched nearby on a log as we approached under the low cloud; in all their black patience, their feather rufflings matched the pace of our amble and their bony nostrils breathed the same kelpy breeze as our fleshy ones. And when we got close, they showed due respect for us apex predators and flapped their wide, heavy wings up to perches on the crumbling cliff.

Vince told Willie about a very successful travel photographer they both knew and whom he'd just seen at a dinner party. Quite powerful, Vince said of her, a woman of real force and ambition. Picking up stones and skipping them in the tidal film, he explained how she had traveled all over the world, through Nepal, Tibet, remote spots in the South Pacific, all over Africa. Apparently she always chided Vince for his endless returns to a group of islands off the west coast of Africa, for his failure to ever go anywhere interesting, like Africa itself. He'd been flying to that little Atlantic archipelago for twenty years now; loved the population's blend of old Moorish pirate stock, African slave castaways, and Spanish sailors. "I don't *want* to go to Africa," he said to us. "That's why. Generations of people have survived without ever going to Africa, right?" He seemed quite bothered by the suggestion, by the challenge it offered to his sense of these daily walks themselves as all the travel a person should ever need. Of course I agreed, and assumed Willie did too; but Vince seemed embattled nonetheless.

When we finally got a good view of the reef, Willie saw Vince scrutinizing it. "Let me guess," Willie said, "it was five times better yesterday."

Vince smiled and didn't answer. We took off our clothes where a few big chunks of sandstone protruded from the beach, pulled on wetsuits, and paddled out to a wave formed by the submerged underside of some vanished point. Breaks usually reflect the very outline of the continent or the flow of watersheds—tide-scalloped sandbars, the underwater projection of a cove's curve—but these waves broke straight into the beach, their reefs remnants of a coastline that no longer existed. The word *reef* is also used in mining to mean a lode or vein of ore, and in sailing as a verb for reducing sail surface—certainly a rock reef does, in a sense, "reef" in a wave. The name Chums just added to an already heavy aura around the place: a shark mauled a guy here a few years ago, and all that chumming for high-paying "eco-touring" clients had stirred huge local controversy; the dive master received anonymous notes swearing that the next time he dumped chum they'd hack off both of his legs, performing upon him, in essence, the core of their own shark fears. I applauded the intent if not the means. After all, the chum flowed with the currents, made a blood slick that sharks followed for days afterwards with their appetites aroused but not sated. And we found out later that a boat chartered by a television science show was offshore chumming that very day.

Diffuse sunlight penetrated the high clouds and rippled across the sea like a streetlamp shining on a river. The waves were surprisingly powerful: coming out of very deep water, they were no more than three or four feet high until they caught the reef. Then they stood up to twice that height, and even as the lip feathered, a second lip formed about a quarter of the way down the face, so the whole top of the wave lurched over in a phenomenon known as doubling up. After the steep drop, which I could barely make, you had to charge to make the hollow wall; the new board felt fast and loose, oddly alive under my feet. Willie and Vince got repeatedly tubed, then came flying onto the shoulder grinning from ear to ear.

"*Formidable, non?*" Vince said, turning to go on yet another great wave.

"Shrackable bowls," Willie added, referring to the hollow bowls forming where the wave heaved over.

"Yolla bowly," Vince yelled back. "The Bowlshoi ballet!"

I couldn't find my way into the tube, and Willie explained that you had to take off on the far side of the bowl, then race across it as the lip pitched overhead—in a phrase, "You gotta backdoor it to get your coverage." The problem was that if you mistimed it, you became one with the lip and participated wholly in its contact with the shallow reef. But we settled into a cycle, taking turns, not talking much, riding in and paddling out, and there was something about the still water surface that let you feel fine gradations of density and resistance. Vince was in heaven, not being the climber who lived for the biggest wall, the surfer who yearns for the ultimate, huge wave; he just sought reasonable, daily perfection, took pleasure in a simple afternoon on a good wave. There were no dragons out there he dreamed of slaying. There's a wonderful way in which surfing falls outside the narratives of death and change—makes, in fact, no story. In all its talk and writing, one rarely hears of the act itself. Three hours of the greatest surf of your life amounts to just that—no yarn. One goes out, comes in, surfs in circles, and spends the vast bulk of the time floating, waiting, driving around. One can declare the rush of the drop, but will be hard-pressed to describe how much water is moving, the feel of different motion vectors, the wild vitality of it all. One can talk of carving deep, then gouging the lip, but even if the listener *can* visualize the living pulse of the wave, imagine the thrill of responding to a supranatural flux and pulling out as it booms onto an inside reef, it still doesn't make a story. The broken truck axle and six-hour hike through the Baja desert for help are far more likely to be repeated years later than how "I made this superlate drop, and then the wave hit that inside bowl and just throated me."

A surf session is, then, a small occurrence outside the linear march of time; sure you can catch your last wave, but rather than a natural conclusion to a well-lived tale, it will simply be the point at which the circle was snipped. So one hears instead of conditions—like a good west swell and light offshore breeze—solid overhead peaks wrapping through the inside. No conflict, no crisis and resolution; no difficult goal obtained or struggle between teams or even with oneself. No obstacle surmounted against great odds—in fact, the hardest part in surfing happens before you get to your feet. Talking about it to nonsurfers becomes much like saying, "I went out and masturbated today, and it felt great." Who cares? The rich tradition of surf storytelling has more to do with what guys did before and after surfing than with the surfing itself, except, perhaps in the case of enormous, dangerous waves. Certainly, anyone can relate to the joy of clean water—birds, fish, dolphins, seals and otters and maybe sharks, kelp drifting with the swells, popping its sea-hag heads up here and there—and perhaps one can picture the crystal curtain falling all around or the wild freedom of gliding into the golden ball of a dawning sun, but still, no yarn. Thus, the tendency toward an "If you have to ask . . ." smugness, inarticulation as elitism: "Only a surfer knows the feeling." One often hears surfing compared to sex; quite a stretch, except perhaps in the unself-conscious participation in a pattern of energy, in a constant physical response to a changing medium—at its best, emptying your mind of past and future. Willie later described it to me as having the quality of Japanese dancing on rice paper, in which the dancer steps so delicately that the paper never tears, and pointed out how each wave washes away all that has come before. And that day at Chums, while paddling back out from a wave and feeling the glow of a glorious ride, I noticed that I couldn't remember anything specific about the wave, couldn't even picture the unbroken wall as it rolled in.

At dusk, all of us exhausted and sloppy, the sun rippled and curved behind the clouds like a bloody clamshell in a gray pool. North over the offshore island, a first patch of blue framed a chunk of rainbow, and then the sky cleared overhead and a huge bulwark of white mist glowed pastel rose. Willie caught a last wave, and as I waited for mine, I thought how awful it would be to be bitten in half after deciding to leave—like a cop getting shot the day of his retirement. But my last wave appeared as a quiet gift, shimmering and silver-smooth, with no roar, bellow, or bite; I soared for a hundred yards on a wall I could barely see. A warm breeze drifted off the cliffs as we stood on a platform of shale taking off clammy wetsuits, pulling at wet rubber and thrashing to get each limb free, and I had a pang of guilt, though for what, I had no idea. Not moving forward? Losing time? Missing life's train? "We going to get penalized at Heaven's Gate, you think?"

"Nah," Willie said, "God doesn't care about stuff like this." Unfortunately, his age rendered the assurance less than convincing; whatever it was he'd needed to prove in life, he'd apparently already proven it.

I looked anxiously at Vince. He just blew air through his lips as if to say, No Fucking Way. Declaring an unequivocal right to enjoy his chosen life. Above us on the cliff, a big, gold-breasted hawk sat perched on a knob of rock. It had grounded for the sun's final setting, coming out of the arboreal for a moment terrestrial, staring out to sea where that gentle blue faded into the very edge of the world. Hard to blame the hawk for such rapture; void being, after all, a function of one's (in)ability to make order of the space in question. And later, as we drove home, the full, purple moon rose over a bay fading like a Japanese mountainscape of misty, forested shores. The color and very face of water seeming no more nor less than wind: some winds are gorgeous, others, aggressive, chaotic, or sickly, but that evening's offshore was pure art. And as Vince and Willie talked about camping up here twenty years ago, when only a handful of surfers knew these breaks, I decided there was something of the New Englander's affection for autumn in the Californian's for surfing—an American sense of place and region. Old-timers always recalled the sheer number of boyhood summers spent under a now-befouled pier, the teenage nights on beaches now buried in condos, the way they truly *grew up* at a now-famous break; as if to say, I am more a part of this life than most Americans are of any life anywhere. A profound insistence on authenticity, a way of believing in an identity our culture does not reward and—as of the climber still in Yosemite twenty years later—asking understanding of values and disciplines that don't answer our sense of what one does with a life.

Winter

Some lucky day each November great waves awake and
  are drawn
Like smoking mountains bright from the west.

ROBINSON JEFFERS
"November Surf"

14

Winter here is a deep, cool amniosis, not at all a death before rebirth—a dusting of snow might sit on the hilltops through a week of seventy-degree sunshine, then wash out in a month of nonstop downpour. But rather than a dead time, like an East Coast winter or California summer, the drenching just gets everything moving toward growth. And the big low-pressure systems spiraling off the northern Pacific churn up nearly constant northwest swell, as long as a local California high pressure keeps them all rolling across Oregon and into Idaho. But once that high pressure breaks down over our heads, the storms swing along the coast and put the wave fetch right on top of us: *no bueno*. Everything messy. On one such day of slopola, Willie actually happy to make a few bucks and Vince actually holding office hours or surfing somewhere he wouldn't tell me about, I made my Point run with a storm just clearing, another dark cloud reaching into the sky from behind the hills. A new finger of weather, the cloud's occasional raindrops hit yesterday's puddles and rippled a reflection of clear sky. New yellow mustard had popped up between storms and painted the hills with a smattering of cheer among all the hard, arid green, and even the marsh hawk stayed low over the sodden remnants of the hemlock. Swallows chirped a bit in the muddy fields, not as thrilled as they'd be in a month or two, just talking and bouncing over a runnel of water along the trail. Little thistles and ferns, newly green and alive, smelled of exuberance amid rot, of tumescence and blooming as the very grass swelled. Out in the water, I rode a few small, disorganized peaks. A pod of dolphins swam by and waves stopped coming. It became very quiet, with just the caw of a gull, the slosh of a surfacing loon—strange after the waves' din. A big hunk of kelp seemed humanoid, and green succulents hung like moss off the cliffs. Seaweed smell, clouds smearing in spirals and sheets . . . so strange not to see a single otter, seal, or sea lion. The dolphins were long gone and I was loitering in the food chain. When a big shark surfaces, they say, one sees first a "footprint" of surging, displaced water—much like the boils welling up all around. My bladder began to complain as I remembered the great white's tremendous sense of smell, discerning mammalian urine at one part per ten million. (How often is peeing a genuine surrender to fate?)

Shark thoughts led my eye back to land, where a stand of slate-gray Monterey pines towered on the bluff, thick and breeze-worn trunks with spare, broad limbs: no fluttering leaves or undignified capillary branches. Death entirely forgotten, I watched them not watch the water they'd not watched for twice my lifetime and wondered how this somber copse of trees bent from decades of prevailing winds could assert daily to me, here in the water, a palpable peace, an anchor of stately sameness. Because it did, lately, the way a certain temple's aspect toward an urban river might let a native ignore, year after year, the changing mix of street garbage and even the clergy's lamentable choice of new stained-glass windows. The way those trees leaned southeastward without any visible shove conjured now a quiet and properly paced passage of time; as if to say, You've found what you needed—waves will continue to break below these trees and over this reef and will continue to give whatever it is you imagine they give you.

Much, I suppose, as would another man's fly-fishing stream or ski trail, a place whose geometry has been imprinted enough times on his eyes to keep him ever at its imaginary center. Funny, too, that just walking up here for a look each day would never have brought me to accepting this one cove as my lawfully wedded life: that came only in drifting hard enough in the very wind warping those branches that I needed a kelp mooring wrapped around my thigh.

I know this because, a few days before, on yet another of several weeks of miserably rainy afternoons, I had walked up here just to taste the coast. We hadn't had much ridable surf, because of the storms being right on top of us—it's best when they're a few hundred miles off, churning up groundswell without disturbing your local surface water. But that day rain fell on stormy water and driftwood lay everywhere on the beach, with bits of Styrofoam and a green bottle. Slipping down the trail, I'd noticed a cross planted in the sand, two pieces of driftwood tied with a strand of seaweed, facing the ocean. As I looked around, I realized someone had left a total of nine crosses along the sea (in the human compulsion to make order of entropy and entropy of order), and it looked so hopeful—a tender little sign of God looking at all that awful evidence. It struck me as a gesture I would never have made, but it also led me to a nostalgia for what life here might once have been. So today, floating on polyurethane foam wrapped in fiberglass, in a neoprene suit with zippers and Velcro closures, I looked back at the beach and marsh and imagined fires among tule-reed huts, a pile of bird bones and oyster shells, perhaps a woman poking among the tide pools and filling a basket with shellfish. Call it the American's curse of always imagining this world without us, but I couldn't help it—pictured boys stripping meat from a beached whale while a grizzly loitered and a nine-foot condor circled, men hunting ducks in the marsh while others pit-baked mussels and ground acorns. Perhaps a man in a reed boat (Quiroste, Ohlone, Hordean?) spearing fish, right where I waited for a wave. Nomadic within a small territory, they migrated a few miles here, a few there; from shellfish to river salmon to acorns in the hills and seeds in the meadows. Extolling the need for such travel, Bruce Chatwin writes in *The Songlines* that "natural selection was designed for us—from the structure of our brain cells to the structure of our big toe—for a career of seasonal journeys on foot." I wonder if our definition of a journey hasn't become defined by its current technological possibilities: we hardly call it travel anymore unless it involves jet flight to another time zone, preferably another continent. But certainly there's something of the slow cycle through one's home turf—such as that advocated by Vince—that answers the need for seasonal movement. After all, during each coastal season, swell and wind come from very different directions, and between the northern and southern borders of Santa Cruz County lie reefs and sandbars that break well on virtually every variation. One turns slowly from break to break through the year, from a particular high-tide beach and low-tide reef in fall, to a different combination in winter, to yet another in spring and summer. Our seasons are too subtle for this to be hard and fast—we get summer conditions in February and occasional northern storms in May—nevertheless, the surfer who keeps alert and searching sees nearly every inch of thirty miles of coastline in the course of a year. It's as if the local surfer's life were at once Thoreau's celebration of the world at one's doorstep *and* Chatwin's perpetual globe-trotting (just with a small globe).

And the Ohlone version of this drift makes a compelling Eden: the occasional warfare costing few lives; so much food and so few possessions as they built new huts and boats after each little move, gorged on the delights of the season. In the 1880s, José Espinosa y Tello wrote that their lives were much like the perpetual vacations witnessed by voyagers in the Pacific islands. Striking a distinctly colonial note, Tello notes that because "their wishes extend only to a desire to have food for the day without exerting themselves too much," they display "an extraordinary slackness and languor, so that they pass their lives in perpetual inaction and idleness, and regard any work and exertion with horror." (Isabella Bird and Hiram Bingham would've concurred.) But certainly the present has its value: while hundreds of right, sperm, and humpback whales no longer loll among the kelp beds, and millions of herring no longer hinder bay navigation (in 1863, an immense herring shoal committed mass suicide, stranding itself ashore and covering three miles of Santa Cruz beach two feet deep in dead fish), at least otters, sea lions—whose genitalia were dried and exported to China to restore the vitality of the aged—and elephant seals, all hunted to near extinction, have rebounded. And even the Ohlone—lithic drifters along the Pacific edge—managed their realm; they scorched alluvial plains to keep down tree growth and harvested the intertidal zones. On slopes where pumpkin patches now turn orange in the fall and European mustard was just now blooming yellow, onshore breezes once fanned Indian-controlled brushfires. Ohlone life ended soon after the missionaries arrived: population at contact was around 11,000; by 1924, it was 56. Malcolm Margolin, author of *The Ohlone Way*, writes that among the little remaining of their culture is a line from a song. The line makes perfect sense to me as I surf here before so much space: *dancing on the brink of the world*.

Another way of putting my primary question: how does a Scots-Irish surfer end up at the end of the twentieth century a citizen of the far western coast of North America and believe in it? Indian thought suggests a nice antidote to our madness, but only the madness is ours, so part of the answer has to lie in the walkabout stories our culture tells: ecosystems and biomes, of course, and even native places of worship, but also who killed whom, what they ate, what they said when they first saw. So, off to the library to look into the white guys who got us here, to pick a false originary moment: try 1542; before anyone built a city on a hill in New England, Juan Rodriguez Cabrillo anchored his small wooden ship off present-day Monterey. He'd set sail from Navidad in Spanish-held Baja California at around noon on Tuesday, June 27, heading along the California coast to China to open up new markets, fill in some blanks on the map, and become the first European to see this beautiful bay, these private coves and beaches. Perhaps Cabrillo and his men were thinking of a northern, gold-filled Azteca, or of the fictional knight who landed on an island called California inhabited by gorgeous black women who let him ashore only to reproduce—the gallows version of El Dorado. Cabrillo's ship drifted north past the bleak desert beaches of Baja and watched the coast get greener, month after month; they saw huge herds of sea lions, kelp beds, sea grass along the ocean floor, and very few Indians. Rounding Rosario Bay and Baja Point, Cabrillo's ship *San Salvador* entered truly uncharted waters. Along the way, Cabrillo stopped occasionally to claim possession for the King of Spain, probably as had Ulloa inland, by placing a hand upon his sword and announcing to the silent forests that he was ready to defend what he had done. Slashing pines and moving stones from one place to another, taking water from the sea and pouring it upon the land—pissing on the proverbial tree.

Everywhere, Adam's task: naming points and bays and islands for the saints to whom the days of their discovery were dedicated, a way of thanking those saints for their direct, indispensable help in keeping the explorers alive. Leaving a legacy of Spanish proper nouns far more pervasive in today's schools, streets, and towns than those of the Founding Fathers ever were. Cabrillo made it clear to Point Reyes fifty miles north of San Francisco, a magnificent headland broken off the mainland by the San Andreas Fault. He named it Cabo de los Pinos for its now-vanished forests of redwood, fir, and pine. Amazingly, he missed the crown jewel, the entrance to San Francisco Bay—perhaps it lay obscured by fog—but didn't turn back until they reached the mouth of the willow-lined Russian River. On November 16, heading home again, the ship rounded the Point at Santa Cruz, where a northwest swell peeling across reefs and tubing over sandbars kept them from coming ashore; they named the bay Baya de los Pinos in another inspired moment (like the genius who thought up the name Half Dome). Days later they drifted south along Big Sur (*El Sur Grande*, the Big South), where the coastal range drops right to the sea, and reported snow-covered peaks and sea cliffs white with ice—evidence of a climate very different from today's. Spooked by the prospect of the oncoming winter, they pushed farther south and anchored on an island off present-day Santa Barbara. While repairing their leaking ships and resting their miserable men (cold, scurvy, ill-fed, exhausted), they were attacked by unfriendly locals; Juan Rodriguez himself decided to help in the fight, but the broken shin he suffered while leaping ashore later cost him his life.

From the time Cabrillo's ships returned to Baja, the Spanish claimed the West Coast by right of discovery. Fair enough, no? I mean, they'd *seen* it. And later in the sixteenth century they sent a few other venturers: Francisco Galli, returning from the Philippines, had orders to poke around for a safe west-coast port; he stopped briefly at Pillar Point, current site of a North American Air Defense Radar Station. Pillar Point arcs sharply south, offering good protection from northwest swell, but if it didn't strike Galli as a likely harbor for the empire, perhaps it has to do with Pillar Point's being the only place in Alta California that sees thirty-foot storm surf; maybe, just maybe, he passed by on a day that the deep-water reef known as Mavericks was, as we say, "going off." And, in 1594, under similar orders to find a safe port for returning Manila galleons, Captain Sebastián Cermenon wrecked his ship on one of the Farallon Islands, in shark-infested waters just outside the Golden Gate. He and seventy others made it to Drake's Bay, where they hacked a boat out of a tree trunk. I love to imagine their stupefied wonder at the virgin stands of three-hundred-foot coastal redwoods, the weeks they must have spent on this lost shore, chopping and carving, avoiding grizzlies and hunting elk. Crowded inside that hollowed tree, starving, stinking, and dying, they sailed (get this) twenty-five hundred miles to Acapulco, riding northwesterly wind and swell past this very reef, just outside the Point's kelp beds, among thousands of southbound whales. No doubt they even drifted into Monterey Bay for fresh water, sailed through those shoals of herring and saw antelope grazing on dune grasses. The bay must have seemed a vision of paradise: a warm coastal lowland surrounded by green mountains, several big rivers making huge lagoons before emptying into the bay, smoke perhaps rising from countless Indian villages.

Three months after Galli's return, Sebastián Vizcaíno sailed north into the same great beyond to explore and settle; winds pushed him back that time, but six years later he tried again and made it clear to Cape Mendocino. He too had the no doubt oddly existential experience of naming the world he passed through. And on December 14, after a thick fog lifted, he saw a huge coastal mountain range (just south of Monterey Bay) and a valley beyond, with a river flowing to the sea. The range became the Sierra de la Santa Lucia, the stream Rio del Carmelo, in honor of the Carmelite Friars: though alien and even irrelevant, the names were again given as thanks for blessings that kept the explorers alive. The ships then rounded a high, forested point, which they named Punta de los Pinos—today Point Pinos and the southern tip of the bay—and anchored December 16, 1602. They renamed Cabrillo's Baya de los Pinos for their benefactor, the Conde de Monterey. Of the bay, Vizcaíno wrote that it was "all that can be desired for commodiousness and as a station for ships making the voyage to the Philippines, sailing whence they make a landfall on this coast. This port is sheltered from all winds . . . and is thickly settled with people, whom I found to be of gentle disposition, peaceable, and docile." Monterey, the headland looming in the horizon's haze due south of the Point—that dark, mountainous outline always to my left as I awaited a wave—was on the world map.

One hundred sixty-six years would pass before Europeans visited again with colonial intent, but those Manila galleons continued to cruise these shores, and perhaps Indians occasionally saw a lantern light at night, far out to sea, Indians born well after Vizcaíno's last voyage and dead well before Portolá's long march. No doubt a ship came ashore from time to time for water or to fix a broken mast. Not explorers, but working men: guys doing their jobs, getting paid. A career mariner could have drifted away a lifetime watching a coast that had only a few place-names in his language, passing this very point and watching brushfires silhouette the hills at night. He could have seen the same Indian village nearby three or four times in his life and wondered about the world past which he drifted, the Sierra and Rocky Mountains far inland, Puritans somewhere three thousand miles away warring with Pequots. Perhaps he would have seen Kodiak Indians in their baidarkas—whale-bone-and-seal-skin kayaks—drifting around the Point in a long, silent line; eighteenth-century slave labor to Russian *promyshlenniki*. Just off the sea stack, the then-local otter might have heard a splash in the quiet morning glass, reared up to see the predator, then dove. The hunters would have fanned out across the cove, waited a few minutes until the otter surfaced to breathe; when the whiskered head appeared, a hunter would have screamed until it dove again. And again, until it surfaced panting for a moment too long and was transfixed by a red, six-foot barbed spear etched with hunting scenes and an otter tally. (To the Aleuts, otter was brother, so who knows? Perhaps this unsustainable harvesting troubled them.) As the royal fur of China, robe cloth of the Mandarins, otters were at the heart of future West Coast settlement—Russians taking nine thousand pelts in 1811 out of San Francisco Bay alone, beached Americans on stepladders taking potshots, hoping the occasional hit would wash ashore. Three-thousand-year-old otter bones appear even in local Indian middens: Ohlones clubbed them on beaches, spread nets on kelp beds, or waited for a mother to dive for food—they'd tie a hooked line around the pup's foot, pull to make it cry and bring back Mom. Very good, however, at avoiding attack, otters are smart enough to swim under boats, into rip tides or windward, even among breakers or jagged rocks where boats can't go. Accounts mention them wrenching arrows out of their bodies with their teeth and crying like human infants. Now, the human economy has swept past such paltry resources; only the white sharks still hunt otters, tearing the heads off hundreds yearly without eating them, like the one I'd seen at Chums. So this creature who once slept openly on sunny beaches, then became famously wary of the faintest human smell or sound, has now unlearned some fear.

Those Russians had crossed the Bering Sea into Alaska by the late eighteenth century, and it was their otter hunters pushing south that made the Spanish King Charles III increasingly nervous. To secure his claim, he sent Don Gaspar de Portolá with fourteen Franciscan friars to dispossess the Jesuits of Baja California and establish missions in San Diego and Monterey. Portolá marched with forty cavalry and twenty-five infantry (as well as thirty Christian Indians, for the horrible work of breaking trail and bridging streams) clear from San Diego to here. At a rate of two or three miles a day, with horses that spooked in the night at a fox or a gust of wind, this seems an unimaginably arduous journey. After a miserable crossing of the Santa Lucia Mountains, they stopped where the Salinas River emptied into the bay, and sent out soldiers to find this rumored port of Monterey—they simply couldn't believe that the wide-open *ensenada* they saw was the sheltered harbor about which Vizcaíno had so ranted. For days they searched, and held a dispirited council on Wednesday, October 4, 1769. After mass they decided to push north. Sixteen scurvied men had now lost the use of their limbs; carried by day in hammocks between mules, rubbed at night with oil, they were a lost and disoriented collection of walking wounded and muttering priests, ambling through a near-paradise of Stone Age Indians. Many locals deserted their villages in the face of these horsemen in deerskin armor whose muskets echoed for miles in the preindustrial quiet. Fray Juan Crespi describes the Indians' terror—which one might also read as tremendous foresight—and how they "ran wildly about, not knowing what they were doing. Some ran to their weapons, others shouted and yelled, and the women began to weep. The soldiers did all they could to calm them . . ."

On October 17 the party crossed a river they named San Lorenzo, which runs through the middle of present-day Santa Cruz, the very river off which the Hawaiian princes surfed in the 1880s and by which Fred Van Dyke and other surfers camped in the fifties; the river which separates Seabright beach down my block from the green steel tubes supporting the Pioneer Log Ride roller coaster at the tawdry Boardwalk. (The San Lorenzo still brings a brown current into the bay during heavy rains, still spreads the detritus and toxic septic seepage of the Santa Cruz Mountains along the sand for the compulsive constructions of tide-wood collectors and temple builders, for whoever made those nine crosses in the sand. Sometimes it even drags out a sandbar that forms flawless A-frame tubes.) Then Portolá and his men walked north past this little cove of mine at the Point, and if that October was like so many, there was hauntingly gentle weather, clear skies, sun setting over that foreign ocean. Perhaps they even saw a galleon drifting on the horizon and felt an affinity for the men on board. By October 20 they were near Punta Año Nuevo, camping at Waddell Creek; though they didn't know it, they were on their way to San Francisco Bay. One day a hunting party was sent into the hills and sighted an immense inland estero surrounded by forest, columns of smoke rising from Indian villages, but they imagined it the inner arm of tiny Bolinas lagoon to the north: shallow, filled with birds and seals (where my family used to spend every Fourth of July and on which the Audubon Society now has a ranch). Even the outer San Francisco coast, with the seven white Farallon Islands and Point Reyes in the distance, seemed merely another unprotected *ensenada*. Somehow they never saw the bay mouth, never put it all together. Hostile Indians and burnt-out grazing grasses turned them south again, still looking for a place they'd already found.

Back at Point Pinos, they guessed Vizcaíno's wonderful bay had been filled by sand dunes, and talked things over: food supplies waning, winter coming, and (like Walt Whitman centuries later) they just hadn't found that for which they had started so long ago. On Sunday, December 10, they left a large wooden cross by the bay shore, and on it they carved, "Dig; at the foot you will find a writing." There in a bottle, they left a note (to whom?) with the facts of the expedition. Then they marched the several hundred miles back to San Diego only to be convinced by new charts that they'd found Monterey after all. So they turned around, again. Back at their cross, now months later, they found a ring of arrows stuck in the ground, some of which were decked with feathers, others with fish and meat; at the foot of the cross was a small pile of shellfish. Offerings to a god these mysterious supplicants had every reason to fear, though they couldn't possibly have known. (Had the Indians dug up the bottle, perhaps it would've seemed a miraculous thing; but, then, perhaps there was such garbage at every campsite along the path of exploration.) On June 3, 1770, near where Vizcaíno's Carmelite friars had celebrated mass in 1602, Portolá, his soldiers, the friars, and sailors—a motley crew on a remote shore—established the first presidio and second mission in Alta California. Father Junípero Serra chanted mass and preached, the soldiers fired their muskets, and, at the end of the ceremonies, Portolá took formal possession of the country in the name of the King—gunshots resounding across the bay, Indians watching from the trees. And all of it where, seen from my surfboard, that vague mountainscape yet completed the bay.

A series of facts and dates, the kind of history that only tells who won; to find the sense of wonder about this land that I insist someone in those parties felt, I have to invent for myself some individual footsoldier or friar, imagine him alive to the mystery of that brief moment in time. In contemporary terms, those explorers may as well have been on Mars, so great was their remove from home, so unfamiliar the terrain. Certainly there are still undeveloped mountainscapes or deserts or Alaskan shores on which one can imagine the absence of culture; but a lush Mediterranean seacoast with some of the most fertile farmland on earth? Beaches teeming with wildlife and mile-wide lagoons bristling with tens of thousands of birds? Millions of steelhead salmon surging back into rivers that spilled across twenty-mile-long beaches of fine, flower-studded sand? One shouldn't indulge in a vision of this place as having been in any sense "empty"—humans here for many thousands of years were ruthlessly enslaved by the Spaniards—but what I'd wanted to know was how my culture first *saw* this place, however unadmirably, which is very different from how it was.

When I'd stripped off my wetsuit and packed it up, wrapped my board's polyurethane leash around its fins, and worked my damp toes into my nylon sandals, I strayed along the beach to look again for those nine crosses I'd seen, thinking I might leave a few mussels by one, an offering of my own. Though I found a lovely piece of water-worn green glass, the crosses had all been washed to sea.

15

The wave, ruler-edged in the bright winter dawn, feathered ahead as I flew; cold, wet speed as the lip thinned to ten yards of spray, ready to break. Two toes off the tip trimming toward that shaking fringe, then carving high and, just as the whole wave leapt forward, soaring along the breaking back. And, in that instant's tableau—a telescopic view down a glimmering glass wall below a snowcapped green mountain and a morning rainbow—I became airborne just as a truly enormous dolphin (perhaps nine feet long) exploded from the wave ahead, its shining gray body for a moment in flight. We both hung in the rising sun long enough for me to shout out loud in astonishment and lose all balance, tumble into the foam as the dolphin speared the surface and vanished. I bobbed about on my back, stared at the dark blue sky and tried to think of a God to whom I might say thanks.

But such moments are a dime a dozen in a life by the water, and serve mostly to deflate the day's anxieties. Which was just as well, because as I stripped off the rubber at this secluded long-boarding break, Skinny pulled his truck over for a chat, smiled, shook hands, and we swapped details about where we'd been surfing. We made plans for the next morning that led to yet another hello from the man in the gray fish-leather suit. Skinny certainly shuffled through the seasonal shift in surf spots, and since I hadn't seen him since the muddy-socks debacle, I was happy to catch up. He'd absolutely sworn off the Point, but was happy to take me on a search farther afield; and he made good company, with just the right irony around his relentless surfer chatter to make it more pleasant than ridiculous. I'd finally improved sufficiently to avoid embarrassing either of us—all that time at the Point without competition for resources. The next morning, the air fifty-five degrees in predawn light, Skinny worked through a power breakfast of four Advil, a cup of coffee, and an Indica bong hit while that feline grin of his split his tanned face under black sunglasses.

"Sooooo," he said, exhaling, "good morning, my son. Where we go?"

Sun not yet up, high clouds in the eastern sky reddening with the dawn, he sat in the open door of his tiny trailer and cracked his knuckles. Slipped his toes into worn-out flip-flops. Sipped at the coffee.

"Sharkenport?" he asked. "Shark's creek? Lane? Ooooooh. Indicator's, ya?" I finally got a glimpse inside that trailer, saw more or less what you'd expect: clothes everywhere, a mattress filling most of it, walls papered with cutouts from surf magazines, particularly the ubiquitous islander-woman-in-thong-bikini. We drove fifteen miles north to check his favorite spot—a remote beach also favored for male-male trysts-in-the-trees.

"No good," Skinny said. "Seen it better. See that little morning sickness bump?"

Didn't, but didn't argue. Where to? Ortegas?

"The Lane could be sick." So, about-face and back to town, sun now rising over the Gabilan Mountains, two women in black tights jogging the sidewalk . . .

"Dude," Skinny said suddenly.

Yeah?

"If we're surfing the Lane together, you gotta be cool."

Howzat?

"You just get aggro. Like, I don't want to be associated with you, necessarily. I mean, just don't hoot and shit, all right? Don't hoot at me."

Ever? Why the hell not? Had he heard about my day with the kayaker? My explosion at Apollo?

"It's just," he said, "you got to keep a low profile. I don't think you realize." Skinny surfed crowded breaks, generally speaking, which means he surfed breaks with well-established local pecking orders. And as a guy who spent much of his energy dodging the world's imaginary blows and avoiding perceived grudges, he'd never fought his way into those pecking orders—just accepted his peripheral caste in the surf world.

A little rubber shark lay on the dashboard. Its mouth was all teeth. While he rattled off the breaks we were passing—Chicos, Fresnos, Gas Chambers, Electric Chairs—I staged upward surges on my finger from the deep, imagined the angle of approach that would get that mouth high enough to hit a surfer. The little rubber toy dangled tenaciously off my finger.

At Steamer Lane, cars and trucks already gathering: carpenters, roofers and painters, doctors, lawyers and professors, all having a look before work, sipping coffee, windows up against the cold. A railing separated the sidewalk from the cliff along which the waves peeled. In the diffuse light, sun still behind clouds, someone tore along a clean green wall, breezing along in the dawn—looked great.

"Don't think so."

Huh?

"It's lost the sand it had over the reef last spring, racetrack's not lining. I want zip today. High performance. Something I can slam."

Wherezit?

"Oooooh, don't know. Need something I can shrack, you know? Like that feeling when you just blow, like the whole . . ."—he gritted his teeth, looked tense—"the whole, fucking lip off the entire, just, you know, separate . . . like remove . . . literally, the whole top of the wave?"

How about surfing Cowdoodies? A ripping left beach-break that required a hike over pasture.

"Local scene's too heavy."

"Nobody's ever there."

"But you still don't want them to catch you out there—those guys took a dump in my buddy's pack."

Protected plover habitat anyway—little sand-nesting birds.

Skinny, Skinny, Skinny. He'd been at Berkeley High School just before me, in the late seventies and early eighties. Basketball, weight lifting, petty theft, and green buds. Lots of black speech inflections—the hometown idiom. Dad a poverty lawyer, brothers going the same route, Skinny was hiding out. Even Berkeley'd gotten too heavy: no waves, for one thing, but also too many enemies. With a fierce little-guy complex, he'd fought his way through twelve grades. Still did a hundred daily push-ups and sit-ups.

"To stay in shape for surfing?" I'd asked.

"Nah," he'd said with admirable irony. "I figured out early I was a shrimp, so I figured I'd be a huge shrimp." And he was.

"Look, let's just rush it," I said, looking down at Steamer Lane, hoping Apollo had an early math class. "Looks killer! Totally surfable. Little inside nuggets doing the shuffle, maybe a big drop or two outside."

"Dude, look how many guys are out. Fuckin', probably be all

the local heavies: Floater Brothers, Slacker Brothers, Peepee, Batboy . . ." Two guys with wafer-thin boards scrambled down a concrete stairway to the water.

"Don't let 'em faze you, dude," I said. "Just do your thing."

"It ain't like that." He looked pained by my ignorance. "But where're we going to surf?"

"The Point?"

"Read my lips. I DO NOT SURF THE POINT. Boring and lame. HP. High Performance. That's what's needed."

The Steamer Lane lifers were starting to show up, guys with reputations for spending their disability checks on beer and whole days screaming obscenities at the action in the water. They'd obviously known each other much of their lives, gathered daily on that cliff like farmers coming in to market—mostly for the joy of bullshitting in a pretty place.

Then it struck Skinny.

"Ooooooh," he said, "see way in the middle of the bay? The Dunes, buya! See those two smokestacks?"

Against the agricultural haze of the Salinas Valley hung two thin lines of smoke.

"Which way's the smoke going?" He asked this quickly, quizzing.

Uuuuuhh . . .

"Offshore. Let's go. It'll be shacking."

"Shacking?"

"Green rooms, shelter sheds," he said with a smile, loving the talk. "You know, tubulation."

But . . . but . . . we'd already wasted an hour and a half . . . tide coming up . . . the Dunes a solid forty minutes away.

"You want speed or not?"

Unbelievable. I really took that shark at my finger while we tore south through the beach towns of Capitola, Aptos, then

Salinas Valley farmland, Steinbeck country—surfer as existential wanderer consumed by angst. I mean, life on the road, following the waves—it's all a load of fun, but this driving and indecision and compromising, not to mention this dereliction of worldly obligation . . . although, if there were indeed barrels, I mean, I'd been *dreaming* of tubes lately. Usually, my dreams were collages of anxieties and memories, but surfing inspired wish-fulfillment fantasies in which I launched aerials at will, took off on gargantuan, open-ocean monsters with ease. And the night before, in fact, the shimmering blue sheet of the wave's lip started to throw over me and, instead of straightening out and fleeing, I ducked under. Suddenly, I was in a sparkling, roaring cave, a palimpsest of all the tube-ride photos I'd ever seen. As I shot out unhurt, a Hawaiian surfer in a yellow neoprene tank top—and he was an important part of the dream—made smiling eye contact with me; I stuck out my tongue in stoke and thought, in the dream, "That guy has no idea what just happened to me. He doesn't realize that was my first legitimate tube ride." Tube riding is counterintuitive, except on the most perfect of waves. You're shooting along, you see the wave "go square"—lurching over to break so hard the lip throws out well past the bottom of the wave—and instinct demands getting the hell out of the way. In photographs it always looks like that most peaceful of places, the ultimate mellow; but really, it's the eye of the storm.

Small highway, farms, somebody's kooky castle with a fake train engine in the front yard. Skinny said the Dunes faced due west toward this gargantuan underwater canyon, so northwest swell got less watering down by continental shelf than outside the bay. Then he brought up our mutual acquaintance Orin—now rumored to have a hundred thousand dollars in the bank from those three years in New York.

"I'm not sure I'd trade for a hundred gees," Skinny said. "I don't know. Maybe I would. But . . . ten years of surfing? Nah. No way. Yeah. No way would I trade." Skinny's girlfriend had been worried about him, thought he ought to get a life. His guru at the local baseball-card store told him just to let her know he was capable of physical violence—solve everything. Hadn't worked. Parents? Simpatico: Oregon Summer Trail Crew didn't wash.

"I told them I'd *love* to get a career going," he said, "and I really would, but the problem is, and I told them, I'm really busy surfing. I don't have time. And, anyway, I told them, like, I've accomplished a lot. I mean, shit, I can surf! That ain't easy. People don't realize that." Making the summer's earnings stretch, he never ate out, ever. Not even a bagel. Never a burrito. A true ascetic, though a patently unspiritual one. He'd even salvaged his TV from a friend's garbage pile. "And my girlfriend's moving to Hawaii to teach," Skinny said. "It'd be so killer to get back over there. She'd have like her own place where I could stay, probably no rent. I think she wants to get married, but shit, she says I'd have to get a job. I've got the money to go and everything, and it sounds killer to be in the islands with her, but I'm thinking, damn, for the same amount I could get a new board and wetsuit."

Past beautiful farms in the alluvial plains of the inner bay, Skinny talked recession, how the guys in the high-school class before us got in on the economy before it soured. "After our year," he said, "I swear it all dried up—no jobs." Affirmative action, he explained, kept the Forest Service from hiring white men more than part-time. They laid him off each fall, rehired him each summer. "And that's my chosen career," he said, shaking his head and watching a semi pass on the right, "so I'm screwed. That's it. Twenty-eight years old, and it's over. There's honestly nothing for me to do nine months out of the year but surf and collect unemployment."

When we got to the Dunes, a harbor seal splashed in the lagoon, and broad Elkhorn Slough—a sort of swampy river of lush bottom land—wound back inland with its rusty grasses now turning quite green. A few pickups were parked where a trail led up the dunes. Skinny parked about fifty yards away.

"Why the hike?" I asked.

"Locals Only parking up there. Trust me. And don't go dropping in on anybody."

The sand path was riprapped with dowels; about twenty yards up, we got a view: from a harbor jetty, the beach stretched clear north to Santa Cruz and there were peaks everywhere, shoulder- to head-high and peeling very, very quickly. Just offshore bobbed a ring of white buoys marking the border of the Monterey Bay Canyon, a colossal, submerged rift every bit as big as the Grand and of unclear origin. (Three rivers emptying into the bay—and more or less matching arms of the canyon—suggested old river gorges, like the Colorado's. But lately the theory had been that it was cataclysmic in origin, a function of shifting tectonic plates.) Regardless, deep water unsettles, and the proximity of profoundly deep water unsettles more—one heard of enormous, amorphous life forms populating its lightless depths, vast, drifting jellyfish. We jogged up the beach, boards in arms, and swarms of little sanderlings scurried in and out with the ebbing and flowing foam, legs too skinny to be visible, their bodies appearing to float about like fish. Farther along, near the peak we'd chosen, another swarm flew in the breeze—dark on top, white below, and flying in such tight formation that when they banked as a group, their white underfeathers flashed like a school of tropical fish catching the sun. As we paddled out, three seals took a good long look from about ten feet away. Then one went under and swam right toward us. A creepy feeling: you realize your mobility is in two dimensions, a slug in a field of snakes.

Beach-break peaks shift as sandbars flow with swell and tide; very unlike a reef break, where you always wait over the same submerged stone. We paddled left, then right, then outside, and the waves had an exquisite uniformity to their peel—also unlike reef waves, since even the most symmetrical of local rock reefs suck out here or mush there as the depth changes. But sand under water settles into smooth, organized form, like a denser liquid within a liquid. Skinny kept hooting at me to "pull in," to duck under the heaving sections and go for coverage. At first I just couldn't find the tube, or bring myself to get in its way. But then Skinny screamed at me to go late on an overhead peak, to stand up just as it broke. I took off at an angle, and as the wave screamed right, I got the oddest feeling that the light around me had changed, perhaps even that time had slowed, and then I'd been double-flipped and body-slammed onto the sand bottom. Came up coughing, but thrilled—tried again and again and started to understand; I never made it out of a tube, but each time I ducked under, I got that same peculiar phase-shift sensation. Waves are, after all, forms moving through mass, bundles of energy expressed as curves: when a curve can't maintain shape because of a shoaling sandbar, its energy bunches higher and tighter until it reaches up over itself, remaking the wave form by pushing water out to close the curve; expressing the original arc, but with a hollow, spinning core. In which the surfer stands. The climber never quite penetrates the mountain, the hiker remains trapped in the visual prison, but the surfer physically penetrates the heart of the ocean's energy—and this is in *no sense* sentimentality—stands wet in its substance, pushed by its drive inside the kinetic vortex. Even riding a river, one rides a medium itself moved by gravity, likewise with a sailboard or on skis. Until someone figures out how to ride sound or light, surfing will remain the only way to ride energy.

Then a very big guy—he looked like James Dean on steroids—paddled near and, with great effort not to sound patronizing, asked if I'd like a tube-riding tip.

"Absolutely," I answered.

"Keep your eyes open." He laughed out loud with me, then introduced himself in a warm, vulnerable way quite at odds with his commandolike appearance. He explained that he'd just moved to the area from down south. "You know what?" he said, smiling again.

"What?"

"I'm so stoked, dude." He had a square-cut jaw and perfect teeth.

"Why?"

"Dude. I'm stoked. Because, just being here in Santa Cruz, I can tell I'm turning a corner. I can tell it's going to change."

"What is?" We'd drifted closer together, both sitting on our boards.

"Just the whole way I been living."

"How you been living?" I asked.

"Oh, dude. Just not dealing. Not doing school. I was really good in school, too. I'm going to be a doctor."

"An M.D.?"

"Yeah. I'm really good at that stuff. I'm going to go to Community College for a couple of years, then to UC and get my shit together. Then go to medical school. Five years and I'll be done and I'll be stoked!" He giggled at the thought as though it were a dead certainty, as though saying it could make it true, in advance. And perhaps it could. He told me his sister had inspired him to come up here. She just had her shit together, that's all. A geography teacher in Florida now, she'd gotten the hell out of southern California. He said it was going to be *so* great supporting just himself.

"How do you mean?"

"My dad's just like lost everything," he said, lying down on his board to paddle toward a set. His arms were comically muscular, with bricklike triceps. The waves didn't materialize, and he sat up again. "Dad's just a mess," he said. "It's like all he does is watch TV and sit on the couch. He freaks me out. It like kind of grosses me out how he just like gave up on everything. He doesn't even go looking for a job and I've been paying his rent. That's why I had to drop out of junior college down south. So I could do construction full-time to pay for my dad's life too." Then his face turned from upbeat denial to a downcast admission of his own role in it all; he said he hadn't been doing all that well in school anyway—got real distracted. "I'd go to the library to study," he said. "Honestly, but then I'd get into studying my own thing and spend *five hours* in the library just reading. Reading whatever books looked cool. But I did pretty badly in my classes."

He spun and took off on a hollow, spinning right, ducked into its tube with fearless poise, and then I saw a big fin surface directly before me, held up by a long gray body. Even as I converted the sight into terror, three more fins appeared and they all turned enough for their raked curves to be visible: dolphins. Then, three more, and two more after that—a parade left and right, behind and before, watery-slick and so humanoid in size. A small wave rolled toward me with three warping dark forms submerged inside it, dolphins giving us all a show by riding the constant pressure surfaces deep inside. And one shot along a perfect wall (dolphins, by the way, *only* ride the good set waves) toward the crowd, only high enough for the top inch of its dorsal fin to break the surface and draw a speeding, razorlike line across the wave. Then wave and rider passed under me; I turned to watch the rolling water's back, and suddenly that six-foot body erupted into the air above, scattering golden drops before the sun . . . Showing off? Oblivious?

"Dude," Skinny said, paddling near, "be cool, all right?"

Huh?

"Those guys are giving you stink-eye."

Who?

"Locals over there. Talking a little shit about you."

Four more dolphins, with something even and paced about their fins arcing into the air and down again, like the inexorable sine curve of the swell.

"Dude," Skinny said, intent, looking furtively over his shoulder, "remember, as long as we live, we're kooks 'cause we're not really from here."

16

play (plā)—*n.* 1. a dramatic composition; drama . . . 3. activity, often spontaneous, engaged in for recreation, as by children. 4. fun or jest, as opposed to earnest: *I said it merely in play* . . . 15. brisk, light, or changing movement or action: *the play of a water fountain. v. int.* . . . 46. to occupy oneself in diversion, amusement, or recreation. 47. to do something that is not to be taken seriously; sport. 48. to amuse oneself; toy; trifle . . . 64. play around. a. to behave in a playful or frivolous manner. b. to have promiscuous or adulterous sexual relations. 65. play at. a. to pretend to do or be. b. to do without seriousness.

—*Random House Webster's College Dictionary*

A south wind tore the opaque green sea as cumulonimbus billowed into blue sky over the mountains, gilded above, black below. A flooding creek silted the cove while the tide flushed through rock runnels as if through irrigation ditches. Outside lay seven seals, and one, with a swollen eye, growled as I approached. It had white whiskers and thick folds of flesh bunched around its head. Hundreds of crabs crawled about the tidal flat, scurried every time

I stepped—move an inch, and the world answers. In a tiny pool, exactly one green-toothed anemone, a sucking mouth/void, faced exactly one urchin, its conceptual inverse, a prickly flesh/sphere. The other seals had light fur and concerned panda eyes, and as one scratched at a parasite in its fur, I saw clearly the handlike bones of its flippers. A mother and pup—two-foot black bullet of life—splashed into a pool while the others arched their backs and stretched like humans in tight sleeping bags. The mother watched me from among the breakers, rolled and faded, kept an eye out. People like me used to harvest people like her. The Greenland method, for example: harpoon a seal from your kayak, row in while it thrashes, and jab with a long lance. When it stops jerking, row even closer and knife it. Or, wrap the seals' rock with barbed hooks; when they come ashore to rest, fire a gun and send them scrambling for the water so they'll disembowel themselves along the way. Or, just get a gang to sneak up in the darkness, cut off retreat, and slaughter as many as fifteen thousand in a night. When, in a moment of unexpected sentiment, I spoke to the first seal—intoning friendliness—it yawned, showing sharp little teeth. A gesture Robinson Jeffers, the Carmel poet, certainly would have appreciated. He once wrote of a killer whale's devouring a sea lion as ". . . beautiful. / Why? Because there was nothing human involved, suffering nor causing; no lies, no smirk and no malice."

As I pulled on my own seal costume, rain shrouded the inland peaks, and the mountain's carpeting of redwood tips rippled in the wind; the sun was setting now beneath the clouds and fleecing their underbellies orange. A small crew huddled in the water, not much conversation. Even the cliffs caught the shades of dusk now, the slow boil into evening. The surf booming thick and erratic off the rock walls also had some Jeffers in it: in his "Granite and Cypress" he describes the waves as "White-maned, wide-throated . . . heavy-shouldered children of the wind." Their origin he ascribes to a very modernist blend of science and native symbol, imagining that "The invisible falcon / Brooded on water and bred them in wide waste places . . . / In the center of the ocean." When I looked around at the Point, at Vince riding yet another broken blue-and-white surge, this toying with the pathetic fallacy struck me as odd for Jeffers, but no Californian spent more time watching and dreaming these beaches and bluffs than he, and his poetry does have an elemental clarity. After the First World War, when ideas like God and Progress looked pretty bankrupt, Jeffers gazed at all this inscrutable coastal wild and declared his own noble place within it. He even scorned weak cypress saplings swayed by the breeze like those here at the Point, and claimed to be more akin to the granite boulders: "Like me," he writes, "[the boulders] remember / Old wars and are quiet; for we think that the future is one piece with the past, we wonder why treetops / And people are so shaken."

I thought I understood what it was about those cliffs and waves that seemed to diminish the force of history, but I was also very, very cold. Shivering and tired in the constant grinding of the surge, I watched an out-of-scale set appear, a row of fractured, wobbling, greenish-black walls. I decided I needed a last wave and paddled toward one, took off on the lumpy face and made the drop, carved out onto its gray hillside, skipped over ambient chop and raced past random, unpredictable bowls clear to the sand. Under the cliff, I had to fight harder than usual to get my wetsuit off, like a second skin not ready to molt—bare back flat on the wet rock, contortionist thrashing to free my left ankle. And then I heard a little splash behind me; there, in a rain puddle, lay a small black snake, fallen thirty feet from the world of grass and rodents. (How? Biting at a bug that teased it off the edge? Just taking a wrong turn? Dropped from the clutches of a red-tailed hawk?) It jerked a few times to get moving in the water, then slithered awkwardly out. One or two vertebrae weren't slithering at all. The snake quickly disappeared into the surf cobble, a goner, going the wrong way: no mice in there, no cover from the tide. A disaster, really. Walking barefoot over the sand, I turned to have that last look at the water that nobody can resist. The sliver of reddish dusk backlit Willie and Vince and a few others still out, enduring a lull, their backs slumped. Then, a few hundred yards outside, the placid, darkening plain of the sea shattered as a whale exploded into the air. Its giant form hung black before the dusk, flukes spread wide like open arms. The whale crashed back down almost slowly, so far did it have to fall. Then the water rolled on as before and the silhouette on my retina began fading, mental picture already becoming stylized, exaggerated. But fifty yards north, the water parted again and the whale surged up yet again to fly dark and spraying before the blurred sun.

I waved and yelled at the guys in the water: "Hey! Look outside, a whale!"

Oh, I couldn't believe it, to be in the water near such a thing and not know it. I dropped my board and ran south down the beach to stay in view of the whale's northward path, dry sand slipping underfoot. A hundred gulls loitering at the creek mouth swarmed into the air, and then again! Exuberance? Perhaps, but only if we can take the word to have a neutral, insentient meaning, as of an abundance of energy expressed in hurling ten thousand pounds of bulk into the warm evening air. Legs cramping and the interval between jumps long since passed, I stopped running and walked back the half mile I'd come. I remembered hearing a surfer describe seeing a whale up close. He'd been sitting on his board, stoned at dawn on a smallish day, drifting, when an adult gray surfaced almost beneath him. He told me he was too stunned to be frightened, but that he didn't paddle for a wave for a while afterwards. South in December, north in April, these whales make the world's longest migratory round-trip—twelve thousand miles. Early accounts record gray, sperm, humpback, right, and fin whales so numerous in the bay waters, hugging the shore and playing in the kelp, as to hinder navigation. But while New England whalers were still harpooning by hand, nineteenth-century Californians had cannons and exploding bomb lances. In quiet, shallow Baja lagoons, deep sanctuaries for the breeding leviathans, thousands of calving mother grays were blown apart. Shore stations appeared all along the north coast, little clusters of cabins occupied by a dozen Portuguese men and their families. When shore lookouts spotted whales, small open boats launched from the beach for a chase that might take them miles to sea. If they managed not to get staved, they'd drag a gray back, winch it onto the beach, and strip off the blubber in a continuous spiral, as if peeling an orange. A man on a bluff by the Pacific, in a loosely held Mexican territory, waving flags to compatriots in little wooden boats; and now a nut at the end of the twentieth century, screaming to another group of men in the water. But this time the half-dozen crew members and the shore lookout are, as is perhaps the whale, at play.

At the parking area, two guys from the water appeared, friendly enough and both strong surfers. I asked if they'd seen the whale.

"That's what you were flipping over?" asked a thick guy in a red flannel shirt. His friend chuckled and looked inside their Jeep Cherokee. "We thought you were having a flashback."

17

"Surfing affects your lifestyle," writes former pro surfer Mike Doyle in his autobiography *Morning Glass*, "like no other sport I know of . . . The surf is only good at certain times . . . If you're a serious surfer, you have to design your life around it." Vince had suggested the book, remembered Doyle as an interesting figure. So, I'd picked it up at Santa Cruisin'—a local longboard store and all-around temple to surfing's golden age (which, in the minds of the current wise men, appeared to have been sometime in the mid-1960s, coincidentally when they were all young). In the world of surfing, Doyle's could certainly be called a representative life. He was born in 1941 in Inglewood to a working, single mother, and by fifteen, he writes, he "had already accepted the old [Polynesian] tradition of the waterman" as his own, and "set about the long process of mastering each of the waterman's skills," such as surfing, paddling, rowing, rough-water swimming, line fishing, and spearfishing. All this made for a very Pacific Rim version of frontier manhood, back when surfer trucks were upholstered with Polynesian cloth and guys living in driftwood tiki huts collected Coke bottles for food. Even lighting out for the territories after high school, Doyle moves to a communal Quonset hut on the North Shore of Oahu. Lifeguarding at Santa Monica, sailing to Tahiti in a catamaran, surfing giant Hawaiian waves, swimming the entire twenty miles of Kauai's Na Pali coast, whoring with the power elite of Peru, winning countless contests, and being voted best surfer in the world in 1964, Doyle achieves the life desired, but not without sacrifices.

As friends like Hobie Alter make enormous fortunes on the mushrooming beach-lifestyle industry, with Tom Morey inventing the Boogie board, Howey Sweitzer inventing the sailboard, Jim Jenks founding the Ocean Pacific clothing line, and Bruce Brown making his *Endless Summer*, Doyle never quite does. He leaves a lucrative job with Catalina swimwear because, "today I would be entrenched in some fortress-like mansion in Del Mar, with a huge mortgage, high blood-pressure, and a job I hated." Fair enough. He then founds Surf Research, selling the first surf wax, a fin attachment for nose riding, and surfer granola. But when business cuts into playtime, he and his partners call it quits: "We didn't want to be surf moguls," Doyle writes, "we wanted to get our water time, be healthy and happy." He invents the first monoski, but doesn't develop it, makes Endless Summer Suntan Oil, and *again* sells his share; opens a surfwear store, and cashes out yet again. He even sells motivational tapes for girlfriend Terry Cole-Whitakker, "high priestess of yuppiedom"—no honor in poverty, control your own destiny, prosperity as a divine right. But eventually her growing mysticism drives him on to other things. Two marriages end quickly, and at forty-eight Doyle moves to Baja alone and successfully reinvents himself as an artist, selling oil paintings to tourists. "I've lived my whole life around the patterns of the ocean," he reflects, "and I've taken a lot of criticism for that. I've made a few women unhappy, I've made some employers unhappy, and at times I've made myself unhappy, but I can't help it, I've always known what my priorities are . . . If the conditions are right, I'll walk away from any job or any woman to spend a day in the water with my friends."

Though not a professional, Vince too had lived his life around the patterns of the ocean, scheduling only morning classes in winter so he'd be free for evening glass-offs, afternoon classes in spring so he could work while the northwesterly winds blew. Office hours and appointments were always timed to leave outgoing tides available. Vince had even failed to deliver a final exam once because of a good surf session, but I suppose he hadn't exactly walked away from it. Nor had there been any friends along. He'd just stopped at the beach for a surf check on his way to campus, got a little mesmerized by the empty perfection before his eyes, and forgot all about the exam. Not until he'd left the water a few hours later did he get that nagging feeling. Walking aimlessly around campus, hair wet and sinuses draining, he was suddenly confronted by a very concerned department chair. But that was a rare lapse: Vince had held the same job for fifteen years and had been married to the same woman for longer. While he might have left her in the lurch for the off lunch date, he certainly wasn't walking away.

Still, there wasn't a surf-crazed teenager in the county who got more waves than Vince; he surfed every day without fail, and often surfed twice a day, even in the smallest, coldest, rainiest, most all-around miserable conditions, when even guys with the day off were inside watching videos. I loved being with him, loved our endless conversations and the unshakable sense that this unlikely use of time *mattered*. We spent one day in particular that winter that I remember clearly, just after I saw the whale. Vince sometimes seemed frustrated or depressed while surfing, but usually, like that morning, he beamed and quivered with childlike enthusiasm. As I pulled off into the gravel to meet him, Vince was already running—not jogging, but outright sprinting—down the dirt road. Age forty-five, clean khakis and sun cap, board under one arm, pack on his back, bounding through the fields on a Monday. I honked as I stopped, but Vince just waved over his shoulder and kept going. It was a fine day for flying, I noticed, as two big hawks carved clean, flapless flight lines over all those little rodents, more interested in each other than in breakfast. They dodged and stalled in a winter light that made color and line appear to radiate from within. Frogs croaked in the stagnant puddles along the tracks, and a ghastly pile of dead fish lay in the grass, the garbage of careless fishermen and somehow quite profane: rotting on a plastic bag, flies buzzing about, so close to their sea. Vince was already half-naked in the new grass when I got to the cliff, surrounded by the little yellow oxalis blossoms that sprinkled all the thistled seed rows.

"Well," he said, looking at me with disdain, "will we be dilly-dallying any longer?" He quickly brushed off his wetsuit, reached into an arm and pulled it right side out. "Have you, or have you not, observed that these lovely little waves are going entirely unmolested?"

It was true, not a soul in the water, but the tide was still a little too low.

He damned himself as we scurried down the path: "My poor neglected wife," he said, "to be married to such a delinquent malingerer." Then he turned back to me, admonished me to haste, and said yes, the tide was, as yet, a bit low, but that the push should soon begin to give the waves more muscle. A storm had ripped the overgrown kelp off its moorings and heaved it up onto the beach in rotting, stinking piles of stranded subtidal forest. Our feet sank into an offgassing bed of decaying sea life, and beach hoppers and sand fleas exploded up in clouds that quickly hid again in the wet shade of the pile. A small niche, theirs, a narrow livable world. Buried deeper in the weed were crabs, spiders, worms, and sponges, all dying their seasonal deaths. A crowd of little white sanderlings rushed out along the border of the draining wash, poked into the sand like woodpeckers into a tree, then scampered back before the returning foam; movement much like the autumnal clouds of sparrows in the Northeast, a body without a head, reeling in response to some matrix of wind and reflex. My grandmother, before she died, told my father she'd always felt like one of these tiny foragers, scurrying back and forth after who knows what. Dad himself had told me their names and what they ate. Just after getting married, he and my mom had moved to Balboa Island near L.A. He'd worked at a cement factory, and when the plant closed on rainy days he'd walk on the beach watching birds. Dad had never been inclined toward naturalism—ordered his life through story and laughter rather than the security of a carefully named world—so I found it difficult to imagine the calm and melancholy he'd have needed to be open to such minutiae. But when I saw those birds now, and watched them poke in the sand, I suspected he'd loved the celebration of the mundane in their tiny lives, their gracious, if Sisyphean, survival.

"Derelictus!" Vince said, echoing Willie as we sprinted to get around a big corner of rock.

"Indeed, derelictus in flagrante." We hadn't timed it right, turned up into a dripping cave just as a wave filled it to our hips. Surf lice crawled by the thousands across the slimy black ceiling, and as the water pulled out, rounded, head-sized stones of surf cobble rumbled out like broken bones. Across a few boulders, we passed the foundational platform of an old jut in the cliff line, a perfect jumping-off point for higher-tide sessions. But the tide was low enough to walk clear to the Point and skip some paddling—over wet black shelves and miniature beaches, out into the water to round a rock, then back again, always following the sandstone cliffs. Next to walls of dripping moss, and again a microverse: encrustations of tiny sand caves, tube-worm colonies, their bigger holes now inhabited by purple rock crabs. Millions of young anemones coated another boulder, their wet, dime-sized mouths closed to the desiccating air. Vince said there was more sand this year than usual; it filled cradles in the rock, beached over little gullies. We waded to our waists between two crumbling, guano-covered sea stacks, then up a natural staircase of little ledges to the very front of the Point: a floor of striated, pitted stone below loose cliffs hung with purple-blooming ice plant. Then, the remnant of the recently fallen arch: a sixty-foot tower of sediment, absurdly cut off from the continent, top grasses dwindling, rodents no doubt fled. High tides had already washed away the bridge's debris, and its remainder stood as an eroding earthen totem, a core sample of the alluvial plain. Someday, it would be shale bristling with barnacle and bivalve, eventually a submerged reef.

Once, after a dawn session just north—soaring straight into the blinding orb of the sun, paddling toward front-lit surfers who glowed golden against a stormy-black western sky—I had taken a wave to the beach and grabbed my backpack. It was a gorgeous Sunday morning without a soul on the mile-long white strand, and I'd climbed up to this same tower. At its base that day lay a six-foot decapitated cylinder of exposed organs, torn muscle, and shattered bone: an elephant seal slaughtered by a very big shark. Sparrows overhead, a few wildflowers fluttering around an old farming windbreak, and only the sound of the sea, a white noise one stopped noticing. But no carnage today as we climbed the tower's side and walked out its base rock to yet another separate little planet of life: the splash zone, never truly submerged, often dry, supporting organisms that needed only occasional wetting. Bird detritus lay everywhere: guano, downy gull feathers, bits of garbage brought over to eat from the nearby municipal dump. Tide pools filled eroded places in weaker strata of the upended rock, and giant green anemones circled these micro-verses like gargantuan maws fringed with hundreds of living, adhesive teeth.

Small crabs scrambled carefully among them, prying at mussels. (The anemones had planted themselves, but were not fixed, could slowly migrate, as could the turban snails, the little conical shield limpets.) An ancient-looking gumboot chiton, red-backed mower of sea moss, was out of place here in the sun—Costanoan food.

Vince put down his board to stretch, looked constantly back at the cliff in rapture at the break's vacancy and gripped with fear of someone coming. He thought he saw movement along the trail: "Interlopers?" he asked.

I looked. "Nope."

"No lope?"

"No lope."

"True No Lope Mutual Fun?"

Vince was notorious among his many close friends for two things: first, a voracious appetite for waves. He'd compete relentlessly for every wave, even resort to aggressive and dirty tricks among friends; it kept you scrambling for your share. Second, he had an almost pathological tendency to swear that wherever he'd just been surfing (without you) had been perfect. Definitely better than wherever you'd been at the same time. Even if you showed up only an hour after he did, you could count on hearing how that hour had been the best hour in years. This all meant more to Vince than just having fun; it was a barometer of the very quality of his life. If you got more waves than he, or made a better choice of breaks, he seemed to feel he was losing what little power he had left in the world. Still, it would've taken me a lifetime to learn on my own what I learned from Vince in a year, his exhaustive knowledge of the tide, wind, and swell matrix for every local scrap of reef and sandbar that had ever been known to produce ridable surf. And in spite of his fierceness in the water, Vince was wonderful company: very wry and quite sensitive to the feelings and opinions of others. He knew when he was stepping on toes, and often seemed embarrassed about it. But he never stopped—surfing was the one part of life in which he was giving no ground.

A half mile north, a big set was on its way. No point in jumping now, so we just looked around: out at the front of the shelf, ridges of barnacle- and mussel-encrusted rock reached into the water, intertidal communities exposed by lows, submerged by highs, taking the full brunt of the swell. Spiked purple sea urchins bristled along the walls of a bathtub-sized pool, nestled in the private little cavities they'd carved in the rock. The organic doors of acorn barnacles were closed now to hold in moisture, but at high tide they'd open—lives regulated by the cadence of waves, the impact and retreat. Another set stood up over the now-submerged shelf, boomed into the platform, and sprayed foam against us and into the pools. Vince got impatient, started walking up and down, looking for somewhere to go, irked at the consistency and length of the sets. Then he just went, clambering over the precarious ridges of barnacles. As he stood exposed out on a little knob of mussels, a green wall rolled toward him; he leaped up and it surged under like a bull beneath a toreador, crashing into the rock behind him. He landed in the surf prone on his board and he scratched hard as another wave pushed him into a current, swept him left into a seething soup. Then, a lull, and he made it outside. Board in my left hand, right grabbing mussels, I scrambled down to the impact zone, through deep pools with little waterfalls pouring off terraces, and out onto a barnacled prow. I waited for a surge to roll along the wall toward me, as Vince had done, then jumped. Unfortunately, my board's ankle leash caught on a horn of rock and yanked my board out of my hands just as I leapt. I landed without it in the surf, stuck in the now-dropping water of the boneyard, a depression full of erratic boulders. Two strokes back, I grabbed the rock and lay flat as a first wave impacted my back and threw my board against the stone; another threw it against my shoulder, and then there was a lull. I slapped at the caught leash line just as another big-set wave appeared outside; Vince was yelling at me to move.

The line came free and I almost jumped, but then it caught yet again, so I stretched on my stomach across this bulge of barnacled stone, thrashed at the cord until my knuckles bled, and then realized I'd run out of time. The water level dropped several feet below and the greenish-gray wall swelled and boiled toward me. I took another step up, dove into a cubby hole, and held on as the foam boomed and rumbled over each bulwark. Water hit my left side and tore me off the cliff, just like that—airborne backwards, then falling again into the boneyard with terrible inevitability. I knew if my head or neck hit any of the rocks down there, I'd be in big trouble. But then I was deep underwater, rolling around without hitting a thing; surfaced near my board, pulled myself on, and paddled outside giggling hysterically in one of my reflexive reactions to close scrapes. Vince kept asking if I'd been hurt, found my laughing a likely indication of trauma-induced shock. When I'd calmed down, he suggested I be more careful with my leash.

A six-foot curve rolled through the still water. No accident that it steepened and broke right at a patch of kelp: the weed's holdfasts clung to the same submerged rock that broke the wave. Properly speaking, between friends, the wave was mine, but Vince paddled hard across my bow to take position and I didn't have much fight in me. I just let him have it, picked up the air sac of a feather boa kelp (pneumatocyst, to be precise—what a great word!) and contributed to entropy, popped it in my fingers to feel the little burst, smeared its clear mucous in my palm, and wondered how much trial and error it had taken to mutate such a system: air sacs alternating with leaves, floating the whole plant high enough to photosynthesize. Enough people have told me what a pain I can be—opinionated, self-absorbed, a poor listener—and still managed to love me for my better qualities, that I'm especially sensitive to the value of learning a person's whole story. Vince spent the water time he did only partly because of his love of surfing; the larger reason, and one many surfers also feel, was that he had no choice. No combat infantryman came back from Vietnam delighted by what he'd seen, least of all a resolutely antimilitaristic surfer like Vince. All I knew about his tour of duty was what I'd heard from Willie: that after a year in the field, Vince's antiwar agitation got him six months in a Marine Corps jail. To this day: no veterans' T-shirts or bumperstickers, and few political opinions on wars big or small. He'd occasionally drop something eerie like, "Let me see, how long's it been since I killed anyone . . . twenty years?," but he never got into specifics. Maybe war had nothing to do with Vince's fierce claim to waves, with the way he looked after number one in the water, but it would've been adequate explanation for me. Adequate for several hours daily of staring into the great beyond, rising and falling with the sea, blowing off steam and having some honest-to-God, just-for-me fun in the process. Even adequate for snaking me once in a long while.

A nearby loon spent half an hour trying to swallow an oversized carp, literally having bitten off more than it could chew. The foot-long fish protruded eight inches from its beak, jerking. Every time I paddled out from a wave, the fish was another inch or two down that swelling throat. (Imagine the indigestion! Like swallowing a cat whole.) The otter backstroked past and I caught several small, quick little waves that wobbled over boils and exposed rocks. Then another lull—waiting, drifting, rising and falling, splashing about among these billions of little dramas. At least the game gives one a small enough lens to get a piece of the world into true focus—

shore-fronting lands like these are the oldest natural communities on earth, their cliffs cross sections of layered pasts, geological time scribed between stratified ashes of Costanoan controlled burns and shell middens. And surfing leaves no trace: the carved wall vanishes, the smacked lip falls anyway. I dropped into a wave as a string of thirty-three pelicans bent and waved over swell and trough, then felt a tear, and my board spun out: a fin, cracked in the debacle on the Point, had torn off. But the water level had risen too much anyway. The waves were sluggish now with the extra depth, and Vince wanted to keep today's lunch date with his wife. We both caught last waves and, just as mine lifted over an inside rock, I flopped off. When I came up: two boards. My baby, my "Shaped for Dan," chopped in half. Vince didn't notice at first, just stood panting on the shale and wrapping his leash around his fins. He was looking at me with sheepish curiosity, perhaps wondering if he'd been too aggressive in the water. Then he noticed the tragedy and I saw a small smile; I waited for a comment about how he'd never broken a single surfboard, how you should never do whatever I'd done. He treated his tools like children and never, ever loaned them out. When we stepped into the trail gully, the roar vanished. I could hear my feet. A bird's chirp was clear among the brambles and hemlock, stunted sword fern and horsetails. Then Vince seemed to catch himself. The advice never came, and he mentioned a spare he had in his garage, insisted I use it until I got another.

18

A sickness, I suppose, or so it seemed to my housemates, who considered me a usually serious-minded young man. It's one thing to watch lousy old movies on TV for their kitsch value, but to rent them in threes? To sit around midday, midweek, watching stories that were contemptible even in their heyday, and that nobody liked less than surfers themselves? As I've said, a mind does what it must. In this case, facing another week of rain and having more or less exhausted the stash of surfing and exploration books, chooses art over life and joins East Cliff Video among the eucalyptus trees, declares a private Surf Film Festival. As one might expect a Manhattan store to have plenty of Woody Allen, there's a remarkable trove of old surfing flicks to be rented around here; and, not surprisingly, they tell more about the Hollywood that made them than about surfing. First, surfing and war: with Vince in mind, I rented Francis Ford Coppola's *Apocalypse Now!* with Robert Duvall as Captain "I love the smell of napalm in the morning" Kilgore ordering a young, acid-tripping Californian personification of lost innocence out surfing in the middle of a Vietnam firefight:

"But, sir," the recruit sputters. "Well, I mean, it's pretty hairy in there. It's Charlie's point!"

Kilgore, with Duvall's inimical aplomb, in a line now gracing thousands of T-shirts: "Charlie don't surf!"

But *Apocalypse Now!* hardly qualifies as a surf flick, so I moved on to the genre itself and its true subject: surfing and love, an issue closer to my own heart. Vince's wife, Fran, stood as a shining example of common sense, insisting that she *preferred* he surf every day: it gave her free time and made him vastly more agreeable company, except on those awful occasions when he drove all over and came up empty. And Willie's wife, who had once insisted that surfing was "another woman," recently made a great symbolic gesture by attending a Goddess festival under the divine title "Tsu" (pronounced "Sue"), as in *tsunami*. And my own Susan? Well, she had recently gone so far as to ask the forbidden question: Which do you love more, me or . . . ? So I looked through the classics, including the Pocohantas love tales of *Ride the Wild Surf* (1964) and *The North Shore* (1987), even the true bombs like *Muscle Beach Party* (1964), starring Annette Funicello and Frankie Avalon, with Stevie Wonder's first film sound track. The cream that finally floated to the top was *Gidget* (1959), staging the timeless and hackneyed formula-romance struggle between male individualism and female restraint. The painted ocean backdrop sways in some studio breeze and the panoramic surfing shots—with Mickey Muñoz in a bikini and wig as Gidget—look like they're on a different continent. Bright primary colors give *Gidget* that candy-land look of early color films, and the beach bums are jovial sailors right out of the old pirate films. Sentimental romance plots, starting with eighteenth-century European novels and perfected in the American romances of the nineteenth century, are concerned with one profound mission: making sure nice middle-class kids marry other nice middle-class kids, resisting corruption along the way. Generally that corruption comes in the form of whatever the culture as a whole finds ominous at the time (lower classes, Indians, slaves, pirates, bikers), and surfers fit right in.

Frances, played by the prim, blue-eyed beauty Sandra Dee, is a sweet young thing from an Ozzie and Harriet home who just can't find the right boy. Daddy, being a caring, helpful man, offers to fix her up with the son of a wealthy business associate, but Frances won't hear of it. Like all headstrong, idealistic gals, she wants adventure and *true* love, so, she heads off alone and charms her way into the surfer gang at their beachside temple—Kahuna's Polynesian thatched hut. It's the middle-class nightmare: your daughter hanging out with lowlifes, even taking on one of their nicknames—Gidget. And, of course, she gets the hots for two of them, making it awfully likely that she'll consummate the forbidden romance and marry beneath her station. Her choices are dark and dangerous Kahuna—the much older chief of the surfer tribe—and dashing, taciturn, but younger and cleaner Moondoggie. Gidget and Kahuna clearly have it bad for each other, but while he's terribly handsome, he's also *terribly* committed to surfing. Cooper's Natty Bumppo, the Pathfinder and Leatherstocking, had the same problem: always the obvious masculine hero but never the groom at novel's end. Kahuna looks great in faded jeans, torn shirt, and shredded straw hat, but their love is as impossible, even unspeakable, as the miscegenation of Uncas and Cora in *The Last of the Mohicans*. Right from the start, Kahuna tells Gidget he's a noble savage who's "gotta follow the sun."

"You can't mean . . ." she says, horrified.

"Yeah," he growls, as if admitting a felony, "I'm a surf bum. You know, ride the waves, eat, sleep, not a care in the world."

Gidget, darling that she is, asks just what I'd asked Vince and Willie: "It may be awfully nosy of me, but when do you work?"

"I tried that once," Kahuna tells her, "but there were too many hours and rules and regulations." An embittered Korean War pilot—I thought again of Vince—he's yet another white man gone native. "For them," he says of Moondoggie and the others, "it's a summer romance. For me, it's a full-time passion." This takes a page straight out of John Wayne's classic *The Searchers*: Kahuna's mysterious, violent past having embittered him to the point of perpetual rebellion, making him unfit to wed. Gidget wonders aloud to Kahuna how he can be so self-sufficient: "You don't need anybody," she tells him, admitting how lonely *she'd* be living the way he does. One feels middle-class America interrogating its fringes: wouldn't you rather go out with a wonderful girl like me than drift around alone all the time? Stay home on the ranch instead of hunting Indians? This argument is the film's thematic lodestone: surfing may be sexy and loads of fun, and those surfers may seem tan and carefree and handsome, but they are outsiders and simply *won't* make suitable husbands. Gidget senses that Kahuna's different from other people—". . . you *have* to be to be able to turn your back on the way everybody else lives," she tells him. "Well, I mean, everybody in life is working for some sort of a goal. Well, I mean, you don't have to have a goal . . . Oh, I'm so sorry!"

Exactly what concerned me at that wedding shower—the "goal" issue—but Kahuna stands firm, like Vince: "What's there to be sorry about?" he responds, fighting a savage internal war. "I told you myself I'm a surf bum."

At the end-of-summer luau—with hints of an orgy, but in fact a delightfully innocent bacchanal—clean-cut kids play ukuleles and make out as Gidget pulls a Shakespearean ruse. She gets Moondoggie, her proper mate, to kiss her under the pretense that it's to make Kahuna jealous, and then gets Kahuna—the obvious choice, but much too dangerous—to do the same to get Moondoggie going. The scheme backfires, and thinking that Moondoggie has forsaken her, Gidget yields to the temptations of beach life: feeling utterly nihilistic, hopeless of finding real love, and cut off from the support of her family, she agrees to go home with Kahuna for she-knows-what. He lights a fire, puts on a little jazz, gets a sleazy look in his eyes, and turns down the lights. Gidget even lets down her guard and has a drink. It's a seamy, tense moment—the climax of the film—in which this lawless surf bum threatens the whole middle-class contract. Fortunately, Moondoggie barges in and attacks Kahuna, and while they duke it out, Gidget runs off into the night—our American virgin, saved.

Poor Gidget is so depressed at being back home with neither of her rebels that she forgets about ever leading an exciting life. She agrees to Daddy's offer, lets him fix her up with that no-doubt nerdy family friend after all. And, lo and behold, he turns out to be *Moondoggie*. But now it's "Jeffrey" and he's wearing a coat and tie, going back to college instead of lighting out on a South Pacific surf adventure. Having given up hope of forging her own identity, and having submitted to her parents' version of a good future, Gidget now discovers that Mom and Dad knew best after all, that letting your parents pick your mate is actually the *shortcut* to romance, not its ruination. Losing Gidget and discovering Kahuna's real (evil) nature has taught Moondoggie too what a mistake this whole surf rebellion was; likewise sobering up from his summer fantasy, he has *also* let his parents have their way. And when Moondoggie gives Gidget his fraternity pin, she gleefully trades surfing back in for love, saying about romance what she once did about surfing: "It's the ultimate!"

19

No surprise that Vince took Moondoggie's marriage as an egregious sellout, an abdication of everything worth living for, nor that I agreed with him. This in spite of Vince's being both married and college-educated, and my being the latter and hoping for the former. "*Et tu?*" he said to Willie as we all sped south in a warm winter dawn, flesh and denim crowded on the vinyl bench seat. Boards carefully piled in back, towels spread between each, fins carefully padded; the radio's recent theft leaving us quietly sympathizing with the clogged traffic crawling and smoking its way north.

"*Et moi* what?" Willie asked.

"Kids. Pascale. She still pressuring you?"

"No pressure at all," Willie answered, refusing to play. He pushed his Ray•Bans back up his nose, rubbed his square jaw.

"Give her time."

Willie smirked to himself, shook his head slightly—not a guy to indulge in misogyny for the sake of conversation, especially not at Pascale's expense. "No, no," he said, "we're square on the kids issue." A white Ford truck sped past with a single-fin longboard in back. On its bumper: "One God, One Country, One Fin."

"Square on it how?" I asked. The dilemma certainly loomed somewhere out there for me.

"Oh . . . you know," Willie said, "you yoke yourself to all those costs, and then the little program on the coast starts getting hard to maintain, and . . ."

"When I was a kid?" Vince said, pushing my leg aside to shift gears. "I looked at my dad, killing himself all day so Mom could hang out at the club, have a little lunch with the girls. No part, for me. *Nada*. This whole patriarchy thing? A complete wash. Ask yourself, Who does the work in our society? Who dies early of a coronary? *Not* women."

My alarm had gone off that morning in complete darkness. I'd creaked down the wooden stairs and pulled my wetsuit from a rack by the furnace, anticipating this single most desired kind of day: sky blue, swell up, and the undivided company of Willie and Vince. I toasted my usual three sourdough English muffins, slathered them with butter and marmalade, filled a thermo-mug with Earl Grey (caffeine abstinence having failed), and pocketed a pear just in time for Vince's headlights. The full moon hung in a purpling sky and the eastern Salinas horizon glowed like an earthen ember. Willie was right behind, and parked his El Camino on my street so Pascale wouldn't have to see it on her way to work, wouldn't have to face Willie's liberty: after all, Vince's theory notwithstanding, *she* couldn't just take the day off whenever the mood struck. Willie'd also been leaving one of his boards in Vince's truck so Pascale wouldn't necessarily have to find out he'd purchased two new ones despite financial straits, and that's how we'd gotten onto the subject of *Gidget*, of surfing and love: Vince found Willie's need for deception, in such an otherwise healthy relationship, a symptom more of a societal sickness than of a personal one, of men feeling ashamed of all activity that didn't directly benefit women and/or children. He had, however, insisted we stop at a particular bakery en route: Fran loved their cinnamon rolls, so he got her a few for later, and we loaded up on espresso, which is risky with three high-strung humans in a small car. Then Vince took us winding through a spanking new neighborhood of antiseptic asphalt and uncracked curbs and just enough variation of architectural theme to not *quite* seem like a tract development. He pulled the truck over in front of a two-story gray house with a broad lawn—fenceless, in a Frederick Law Olmsted vision of the suburban green. On the beach below, a perfect little wave slipped across a sandbar that hadn't been there last week, would doubtless be gone by next: a product of silting from the rains, not yet washed out by the downcoast littoral drift. All seemed still, no local surface harassment; the swell came through from afar utterly without static, like a transcontinental phone call with a perfect connection.

"Shall we look elsewhere?" Vince asked. "Or just nip the day's anxieties in the bud?"

"Nippage," Willie said.

Vince squinted north as though one could possibly see thirty miles around the mouth of the bay.

"Don't start," Willie said. "I can't be driving all over creation."

"Nip and tuck."

Indeed: back to the truck, naked in the street. A gray-suited man in a silver Japanese sedan gaped at our semipublic seminudity, and Vince looked pensive, shook his head in pity. "See," he said, "it burns people to see guys like us enjoying the gifts of the ocean while they kill themselves making big bucks just to listen to it at night. Maybe walk the beach on weekends with the spouse in matching jumpsuits and pick up sand dollars."

Willie looked at him with concern. "Whoa there," he said. "Rel*ax*, bro. Just people leading their lives."

"I'm just saying," Vince persisted, downing the dregs of his coffee, "while wifey's showing hubby that starfish, all he's thinking about is his neighbor's cuddlefish."

"You think?" I asked.

"Well, if he's healthy—probably his heart if he's not."

"You drinking regular today?"

A sign blocked the wooden staircase down to the beach: "Trail Closed, Washed Out by Rains." We climbed over it, and as we scampered down a forested gully, Vince called back up that he simply saw all this feminist stuff about work as a big double standard. Asked to be shown *one* woman who'd put up with a man not working. "I'm serious," he said. "Even the most ardent feminists are comfortable making less than their husbands, they're comfortable making the same—though it tests their mettle, to be sure—but as soon as he's making less, she's *out* of there." Bad news, if true: Susan had a promotion coming up that would put her about ten thousand yearly dollars ahead of me. Off the stairs, and onto an eroded dirt trail among sword ferns, willows, and oaks; a lush and quiet gully with the high greenery of a rain forest. The rains had destroyed most of the trail, so we slipped down loose little slopes and stepped along deeply cut creek trenches, now dry. While we walked, Vince asked about Pascale's complaints over the years, and Willie admitted she'd had her moments, saying, "You think the mornings are cold now? Just keep blowing me off when the surf comes up." But she had a point: their cottage *was* cold.

As Vince stepped gingerly around a bush of oily-green poison oak, he paused to think about it. He admitted he didn't give Fran enough credit. I remembered showing Vince a new longboard once, out on his sunny lawn while Fran sat in a wicker patio chair reading a paperback Chekhov collection. She'd looked up at one point and—from behind her black cat-eye sunglasses—asked absently if I'd ever ridden a twin-fin longboard before. This from a doctoral student in philosophy who never even played croquet—much less went surfing—and couldn't possibly have either known how a twin-fin longboard performed or cared. Still, her voice had carried no trace of irony or mockery, no spoofing the boys' little game. Being brilliant with languages, she had simply mastered the idiom, accepted it as a meaningful part of the man she loved, and offered the question as a pleasantry to her husband's new friend.

The gully ended at a long, open beach strewn with driftwood and smelling of kelp. The waves had a green, milky translucence to them—quick and bright little flights, the three of us taking turns. "Friars Nip and Tuck," Vince said, nodding to Willie and me, paddling out for yet another: "Religious zealots, at work." Several hours later we walked wearily back to the car, drove down to a Mexican place for lunch: one-speed fat-tire bikes leaning against a bench, a deck overlooking the blue bay as the Southern Pacific rumbled by and the waitress who owned the place brought rock-cod tacos with homemade salsa and black beans, chips and beers with lemon wedges. At another table sat three young surfer couples, each with a very young baby. A big man with a prominent nose and Adam's apple looked happily bewildered as he twirled his coffee spoon and mentioned yet another surfer acquaintance who'd just become a father. In a nasal drawl, shaking his head from side to side with his eyelids at half-mast, he said, "Eeeev-erybody's haaaving 'em."

Spooning mango-habanero salsa over my last taco, I got to thinking about Susan, how she wished the things we did together gave me the rush surfing did.

"Well, hey," Willie said, "she put her finger on it. You probably wish the same thing."

"That's what I told her."

"You *told* her that? Wow. Cold."

"Actually," I said, "her favorite thing now is to tease me that I *want* her to be pissed about surfing." It was true—she had my number. "She's got this theory now that if she would only get all worked up over my surfing, it would make me feel really rebellious and manly and give me something to complain to you guys about."

Willie nodded in approval and took off his shirt. There's a rare form of midwinter warmth on the California coast that makes you want to pause and say grace: gentle, at once cool and warm, sun not at all threatening, smogless skies so clear we could see wind-rowed trees along the distant Santa Lucia Mountains.

"Dude," Vince said, his eyes rapt upon a surprisingly big row of blue walls that bent away from the cliff and arced across the bay. "Ooh la, lala . . . wide-wale."

"You guys hip to the family psychodrama?" Willie asked, hands folded on his tan stomach. "Where when you're a baby, you look down between your legs"—he demonstrated—"do the same to Mom, and get the bad news: *la différence*. You know this stuff, right, Dan? The male wound?"

I shook my head.

"Mom's your whole world at that point, right? Your universe? And now you're realizing you're different from it. Women don't have this problem, apparently, because they look at Mom and just say, *Hey now*, you me same. No need to justify the oxygen they consume."

"Let's get the bill," Vince said, trying to catch the waitress's eye.

"See, surfing's where the wound comes in," Willie continued. He picked at our third basket of shiny tortilla chips. "The big hole, right? Those empty places inside from the big wound, so, hey—got to fill."

"Pascale feeding you this?" Vince asked, pulling out his wallet.

"No, no," Willie insisted. "See, the theory goes—and you ought to get into this, Vinnie. I mean, a wound? You could finally claim victim status all for yourself! But look, the man gets, from this gaping hole he gets inexhaustible energy for *intimate* obsession, which," he looked both of us in the eyes, "strikes me as a fair characterization of a few guys we know, an *intimate* obsession with nonhuman activities . . . with systems of ideas . . . and *wait*, Vinnie. Don't change the subject, we all see the sets stacking up. Just admit it. You're a pretty wounded motherfucker, wouldn't you say?"

Vinnie was rubbing his eyes.

"And you, Dan?"

I nodded. Definitely wounded. And definitely witnessing corduroy.

"So the *woman*," Willie said, putting both elbows on the table, "that's supposedly why she can't relate to your needing to do your thing all the time. She never got that wound. She never had to say, Hey, *mio isolato*. Just, 'Mommy looks like me, world looks like me.' Keep on getting all that intimacy from other humans. So, they see any *other* focus as somewhat . . ."

"Like surfing."

"Like surfing. Or physics. Or sailing. Or whatever . . . Oh, God, that *is* a glorious wave."

Vince stood up from his chair: "Can we go now?"

Tortilla chips finished, bill paid, cookies and coffee procured at a nearby cart: straight to the actual Point, out that gorgeous dirt road with everything wet and greening, chi city along the trail—foxtails shooting straight up, wild radishes blooming purple and white, little blue bells and mustard crowded among the blackberry brambles. One bush held up six perfect, fully bloomed California poppies, each with four orange petals cupping a bright, swirling fire of orange stamen; all mounted on single green stems with little purple disks just under the blooms—crazily delicate and perfect. And, best of all, there was no breeze, so the surface lay still and the swell mist thickened. Windless warmth only happens a few days each spring, a few each fall: ten such days total, maybe twelve in a year. They make one aware of how busy the coast usually is, hustling its sky from one place to the next, sucking in its fog or bringing a storm on down from afar . . . how parched its plants are in summer, how muddy and sodden midwinter. Those days were the three percent of the year's life cycle when the coast stood statically, happily alive, not rushing off to become somebody else. And as we approached the train ditch, a big bob-tailed bobcat with thick hind-legs bounded out of the brambles and across the road before pausing. It looked back over its shoulder at us with its flat face and pointed ears, the way cats often do: not confronting, ready to bolt. One more step to the tracks, and it vanished.

"Boys, boys, boys," Vince mumbled when the waves came into view, "sea shivers shuddering." He began peeling off his clothes. "Look-look-look-LOOK! Oh, pure, pure . . ."

"Don't say it," Willie demanded.

"Can't I?" Vince whined.

"Don't."

"Pussy?"

"Damn you."

Suited up, we scrambled out along the cliff, climbed up the platform, and stood as if on the prow of the continent, cleaving through the oncoming sea. With absolute regularity of wave shape and clarity of wave line, the moment felt very much like those I'd hoped were implied by those months of "the swell's making no sense." The moment when the place you gave so much love, the reef you'd learned so intimately, finally intoned the perfect speech you knew it could. We waited for a long lull, since getting caught inside one of these sets would be disastrous. When it came, we jumped and scrambled to the outermost peak with dry hair. The waves were nearly three times my height, but the water was so smooth and the waves so clean, one could just stroke evenly until gliding, stand up, and scream down that long face. Near the wave's bottom you'd lean the board's rail into the water and channel all that energy back up the wall, hit warp speed across the bay in long, open airplane turns. The swell built all afternoon, and conversation never resumed: too rarely in the same place at once, too much else to think about, no misery seeking company. The slowly setting sun gradually turned the world into a glassy planet of crimson mist and the dropping tide moved the takeoff spot ever farther to sea: from behind, the wave backs rolling on toward shore made mile-long walls of translucent crystal. When the bigger sets came, they appeared first as dark irregularities in the distance. Vince knew exactly which boil they'd break over, and held his ground every time—resisted the temptation to scramble out toward the incoming waves and thus toward the safety behind them. Near dark, I watched Vince drop down a wave face that dwarfed him and it took a long time for me to rise over its shoulder. Concentration kept him from waving, but he smiled as he soared past. Pulling out of my own final wave felt like stepping lightly off a speeding train, and I was last ashore as the sun's ball touched down. At the patch of grass, Willie was telling Vince how he needed to get home, had a couple of halibut steaks in the fridge and wanted them ready before Pascale got back from work. I sat for a while before changing, looked across that most adored of coves, and felt something rare in a life: the sense that I had been present and prepared for an instant of . . . what was the word I had used? Plenitude?

"The wound," Willie mused, stark naked in the darkness next to his prostrate white surfboard.

"Think that's why you fetishize your surfboards, Vince? Castration anxiety?"

Vince looked up briefly, then pointed out the biggest wave we'd yet seen, standing up and starting to feather. Vince mumbled something I didn't catch, kept watching that golden warp bend and vibe across the reef. Behind the black clouds, the sun's orb bent back up over the horizon to reappear as an orange ghost in the vagueness of the new storm.

20

I once stayed with a friend in a nearly deserted high-rise hotel in Wichita, Kansas, that had a defunct tiki room full of potted palms and thatched-roof bamboo bars. Walking back to the hotel from dinner, through dark and deserted streets, we passed an abandoned parking structure: deep inside, the familiar click-clack of skateboards doing tail slides and rail grinds on the concrete forms. I had an awful night of sleep—our room, on the only occupied floor, pulsed a blood red from the flashing neon clock of an adjacent office building, a nearly hallucinogenic beacon of modernity in all that High Plains emptiness. In the morning, I wandered over to a convention center to kill time, found a car show devoted exclusively to VW bugs. There in Wichita's dying downtown—relic of its muscular days as a cattle capital—on this showroom floor, a thousand miles from the coast, lay a vintage 1970s twin-fin shortboard in the back of a bright yellow convertible. The board's use—its life as a functional tool—was irrelevant to its status as a talisman for the dreamiest American vision of leisure. And not so surprising, really, given that Wichita was the first inland city to see Bruce Brown's *Endless Summer*, the most successful surf film of all time and the next screening in my private festival.

Even if you've never seen the movie, you know what it's about:

southern California, eternal childhood—Peter Pan. Opening in Santa Monica in the summer of 1964, *The Endless Summer* played to sold-out audiences for seven nights. To prove it could sell outside of L.A., Brown rented a theater in Wichita: smack in the geographical center of the country, in freezing winter weather. Smash hit. On to New York and rave reviews—Bruce Brown as "Bergman of the boards," "Fellini of the foam." *Newsweek* called it "breathtaking . . . a sweeping and exciting account of human skill pitted against the ocean." *The New York Post* said the film was "something very special . . . Anyone who can't see the beauty and thrill of it hasn't got eyes," and *The New York Times* declared: "Buoyant fun, hypnotic beauty and continuous excitement." Mike Doyle thought it demonstrated the pure freedom of the sport: "There were no bells," he writes, "no stopwatches . . . just you, a surfboard, and the water. The surfers in the film weren't hurting anybody or anything. They were just doing something they truly loved, something as simple as looking for the perfect wave." Trivial as the film may now seem, *The Endless Summer* grossed $30 million on a $50,000 budget; Brown's home-cooked documentary—*The Endless Summer* didn't even have dialogue, just a voice-over added later—earned him in the neighborhood of eight million dollars. Makers of early surf films would rent auditoriums in coastal towns, sell tickets at the door, play records, and narrate from the stage while the crowd hooted and whistled. And, no plot, no sex, no violence: Robert and Mike just trot the globe for ninety minutes, behaving in wildly alien cultures as though they were still at Malibu. Absolutely no mystical overtones of truth-seeking—just a fifties hedonism of wholesome, laid-back fun.

Much of *The Endless Summer*'s charm lies in the laughter of people startled and thrilled by surfing, in footage of delighted Senegalese children playing with surfboards, pearling, rolling, occasionally getting to their feet. It makes an appealing vision of global community forged by Californian fun. In one scene, a group of Senegalese men paddle an intricately carved canoe out to lay fishing nets. "They couldn't speak English," the narrator explains, "and Mike couldn't speak their language, so they paddled by and said something like, 'Unga wamungi wungo.' Mike smiled and said, 'Yeah, man, hang ten.' They thought that was great. They went stroking out chanting, 'Hang ten, hang ten.' " And later, as they all stand smiling on the beach, the Senegalese surround the Americans and ask untranslated questions; the boys answer in English, and both sides engage in a joyous nonconversation. Play transcends not just culture, but language itself. To a 1990s eye, the film's 1960s colonial stupidity is embarrassing: two healthy, wealthy Western boys on an unparalleled journey of cultural imperialism—the whole world as their amusing theme park. On the plane to Africa, Robert wonders, "Would they find surf? Would they catch malaria? Would they get speared by a native?" In Nigeria, a blackface native chases them through a "full-on jungle where they expected Tarzan to come swinging by on a vine," and at a Senegalese "primitive fishing village," the boys worry that "surfing would violate some religious taboo of the natives and they'd attack." Of those fishermen rowing out to sea, the narrator notes that when "you're sitting outside looking at them paddling toward you, you think they're coming out with their forks to have you for dinner." These oarsmen have no problem catching a few waves in their canoe and are, of course, all wearing T-shirts and jeans. But a world about to blow apart with social and military conflict happily indulged in a last pre–My Lai, pre-Watergate fantasy of a Pax Californica.

And maybe I felt some of that fantasy the first time I ever stood on a surfboard. I was twelve years old, in the fog in southern California—Dad and I were down from Berkeley to surf with Uncle Jim and camp out on the asphalt lot near San Onofre's nuclear power plant. Jim was back from a few years wandering the globe, surfing in Indonesia, trekking in Nepal. A guy who'd surfed Waimea Bay as a teenager in the late sixties, even Banzai Pipeline a few years after it was first surfed by Phil Edwards. When the legendary swell of 1969 hit during finals week at UC San Diego, his roommate had just dropped out—three days from a degree and his priorities straight, conscience clear. And San Onofre, though one of the great early surfing destinations, was too cold that evening to conjure the old tiki huts, flatbed Fords, and redwood longboards of the twenties and thirties; too much pavement to feel the New Polynesia that once was. Nevertheless, Dad and Jim made quesadillas on a backpacking stove, slipped the kid a little Jack Daniel's, and talked about water. I was a pale, urban boy anyway, still more into electric guitar than the ocean but stoked to hear Dad's memory of bodysurfing big Windansea—not another soul out, water warm and clear. My father is one of the best storytellers I've ever heard, and as we ate, he described the sun setting with nobody out but the two brothers, how after several hours of wrapping his body around each wave's internal curves, he'd decided to catch the sunset from a new angle. He dove six or ten feet down, he said, then turned to watch the dusk's pink light shaft green through the waving stalks of the kelp forest.

"Right out of high school," Dad went on, "I took off for Hawaii. It's not like I was a big surfer or anything, but I knew something was happening over there." His own uncle, Johnny Morrissey, had been stationed at Pearl Harbor; Dad heard they had free surfboards for Navy dependents. "So, I took a bus out through the cane fields, and I remember being blown away by this big bonfire burning in the heat, sending the bodies of dead sugarcane workers back to Japan. I learned how to surf, went skin diving, speared a leopard eel. But just to give you an idea of what an idiot I was, I met Miss Waikiki at this Navy social, and the next morning she called and said, 'Yeah, look, I've got this car for the day . . . maybe we could take a picnic out to the other side of the island.' You know what I said? 'Look, I'd love to, you know, but, see, they've got these surfboards out here and I . . . you know. Sorry.' " Sitting there listening, I mulled over having got to my feet that afternoon; just like that little kid at Pleasure Point, I'd had this flash of amazement: *Oh my God, I'm doing it! I'm actually surfing!* And now it mattered to me that my father had surfed in Hawaii way back then; I even found myself wishing things he didn't—like that he'd stayed and lived that life.

Half an hour of freeway lies between Berkeley and the nearest surfing beach, and it's no place for beginners. The landlocked adolescent solution was carving asphalt, skateboarding empty swimming pools in junior high. Tim Heathcliff's mother graded papers at Denny's while we ripped concrete waves, deep pools, freestyle bowls, bump courses, snake runs, arcing off smooth stone walls, into the trough and up again. When Tim realized blue corduroys were a bad choice for ninety-degree Central Valley heat, he skated down to the mall, avoided Denny's, stole some scissors, went into the men's room, and bingo—shorts. Yelling out "Dropping in" meant you were entering a pool; at age twelve, I repeated it in bed at night. "Dropping in!" was an assertion of participation—I belong. Of agency—I do. Summer afternoons at a rooftop tennis court, plywood strapped onto the fence to extend the concrete floor's upward curve: take a few strokes, shoot up the wall, turn, and back down. Off the lip. Then, twenty-five cents and the number 7 Euclid bus to the top of the Berkeley hills with a handful of doughnuts and loads of potential energy ready to go kinetic. Shooting narrow sidewalks on our tailbones, pulling tight, forested turns. In a pinch, you could lay it out into someone's petunias. Downtown again, catch the Humphrey-Go-BART—university shuttle free to students and twelve-year-olds with skateboards—to the top of the campus. Just after dark, we'd disembark, do a bong hit in the bushes, point our boards downhill, and yield to gravity. Surfers say God Must Be a Surfer; the grounds planner of UC Berkeley must have been a skateboarder. Flawless paths of blacktop snaked through groomed lawns for nearly a mile. Cold air in our faces, jeans wearing out on the sandpaper grip tape. "Roller!"—a cop car lurking in the shadows ahead and word coming mouth to mouth. Peeling off into the grass, we'd tumble over and slide on our sides across a wet lawn.

But asphalt's hard: a kid's foot completely backwards in the bottom of an empty pool; Adam Crowley compound fracturing his leg ("Dude, you should've seen it, his whole bone sticking out. I mean, I hate him and everything, but I felt kind of bad for him"); skateboard hero Ivor Brown, jumping off on a big hill to run out his momentum, heels slapping his butt, going down and sliding on his chin like a fleshy toboggan. So I slowed at intersections, was a coward for looking both ways. Reed Deleuth, comic-book maniac and, later, speed freak in Hell's Kitchen, told me how he saw automobile cross-traffic. "Fuck 'em," he said, a Californian through and through, "if they hit me, I'll sue their ass and get rich." And, of course, one who kept at it: Luke Marcus, professional teenage skateboarder turned cross-country ski racer, moved to a town high in the eastern Sierra Nevada. Vegan endorphin junkies, he and his wife would run twenty high-altitude miles most Saturdays and once skied the fifty miles from Mammoth to Yosemite in a day. Weekday nights, two in the morning, she'd follow in the car while he skateboarded down fifteen miles and four thousand vertical feet of blacktop on the June Lake road—soaring through pine-scented alpine air, carving around wide, smooth turns, riding waves in the continental rift into desolate desert sage below the Aeolian Buttes. And when I finally got a driver's license, I drove over the Bay Bridge to San Francisco, past Golden Gate Park and endless neighborhoods of Victorian and stucco townhouses to the concrete promenade where broad Ocean Beach separated a cosmopolitan metropolis from open wilderness. Got promptly beaten up by the shore break and washed back in without catching a wave. Sat on the beach among beer cans, transvestites, and fishermen, and wondered what the hell was the matter with me.

The hook sank for good on high-school road trips down the coast—camping on empty beaches and barbecuing in the sand. The mythos of surfing certainly has its tales of pioneer bravery—the first guys ever to surf Waimea Bay, ever to find that flawless tropical reef pass—but most spots are less than lethal, so tales of who first had the *pleasure* of this wave are the ones that count, how magically clean and uncrowded it was, stories of cheap gasoline and undeveloped land before you and your kind came and botched it all up. More than a myth of conquest, it's a myth of the garden. Witness the 1978 film *Big Wednesday*, taking the surfer's southern California—that of my father and uncle—from 1950s innocence through 1970s experience. First, the paradise we're bound to lose in the "South Swell, Summer, 1962," a soft-lit scene of beautiful young men and women waking up on the beach. Water clear, campfire crackling, a voice-over like Bob Starret's recalling Shane remembers how "in the old days . . . a wind . . . would blow down through the canyons . . . it blew the strongest before dawn, across the point. My friends and I would sleep in our cars and the smell of the offshore wind would often wake us, and each morning we knew this would be a special day." Our three heroes then walk down a broken Greek stairway to the figuratively classical beach: tragic, handsome Matt stumbles along drunk while wild-man Leroy holds him up and blond, blue-eyed Jack demands Matt walk on his own two feet. Silhouetted against the red evening sky stands the temple: an old pier with a shack inhabited by Bear, bearded old man of the sea, guru and board shaper, kahuna. With beautiful, undeveloped hills and a railway trestle in the background—stand-ins for California-as-Eden—a towheaded boy tells Bear how he worships Matt; Bear agrees Matt could be a great surfer, if he sticks with it.

"What do you mean?" the stunned boy demands to know. "Those guys are so stoked they'll surf forever."

"Nobody surfs forever," Bear announces grimly, establishing the film's true subject as he lays fiberglass over a balsa big-wave board, a totem of power. The boys ask when the great board will be ridden, and Bear says, "It'd take a big day . . . a swell so big and strong, it'll wipe clean everything that went before . . ." Act 2, "The West Swell, 1965," ends the idyll: Jack and his sweet girlfriend, Sally, find Bear in a drunken, weeping stupor, pulling down the shack and growling the renegade's litany, "Move inland . . . taxes . . . marriage . . . divorce. The whole damn thing." He cries out, with drool on his lips, that modernity is upon us, that they've condemned the pier: "You'll be living under the booted foot of the lifeguard state," he moans, and the film promptly begins piling up the lives of pain and frustration Bear's prophesied great swell will wipe clean. Jack *becomes* the lifeguard state and kicks Matt off the beach the very day draft notices arrive to a war the movie never names. Matt and Leroy fake medical disability, but Jack accepts duty to God and country, with the Watts riots raging on a just-audible television. Matt opens a pool-cleaning service and marries his pregnant girlfriend, and Leroy moves to Hawaii to pursue the dream. But, as Bear promised so long ago, the sea can bring back (almost) all of what we've lost. Jack comes back from the war an officer and a gentleman (but Sally hasn't waited), Leroy returns from the islands a surf hero, and "The Great Swell, Spring 1974," brings a full seasonal turn of a man's life and the big one Bear foretold. The horsemen ride again: graying old Matt takes off on the Great Wave and soars through tube after lethal tube until a collapsing wall sends him drowning in a netherworld of bubbles. Jack and Leroy leap to the rescue, and, with the glue of boyhood friendship, the three aging surfers hold tight in the figurative maelstrom of life.

The surfer endures on the greatest-hits list of American character types, right up there with the cowboy and the Puritan. Like the former, the surfer is recognized primarily as a Yahoo peasant. Take Jeff Spicoli, played by Sean Penn, in the 1985 *Fast Times at Ridgemont High*: a mindless, preverbal slave to his senses (though also endearing and very funny). Or, even more telling, the media representation of witness Brian "Kato" Kaelin in the O. J. Simpson trial as a "quintessential aging surfer." *Surfer* magazine reports that Kaelin, from Milwaukee, had never so much as set foot on a surfboard; he got the newsroom title, apparently, by being blond and inarticulate. The surfer also made an easy and natural target for Tom Wolfe. After the success of his first book, *The Kandy-Kolored Tangerine-Flake Streamline Baby*, Wolfe undertook the kind of journalistic pilgrimage that always makes its subjects cringe: a report on our eccentric provincials. Wolfe's surfers in *The Pump House Gang* (1968) lead an all-star cast of eccentrics: big-breasted Carol Doda, *Playboy*'s Hugh Hefner, slumming English socialites. Teenage disdain for the aged—including, presumably, thirty-something Wolfe himself—dominates the piece; the only description of surfing comes from Jackie Haddad, "daughter of a certified public accountant." Rather than try it himself, Wolfe excerpts her story with contempt, telling us that she "wrote it just for herself, called 'My Ultimate Journey.' " A beautiful description of big Windansea, but for Wolfe it's just local color. He does describe two guys in the water, offers that they're "staring out to sea like Phrygian sacristans looking for a sign," but even this he reduces to its social cachet: not a pursuit in its own right but "a glass-bottom boat" that "floats over the 'real' world." (Surfboard envy?) Wolfe also writes that the surfers refer to "the mystery of the Oh Mighty Hulking Pacific Ocean and everything" as "mysterioso," and yet it doesn't occur to him that this could be more than a pose. He tells the story of Bob Simmons's death in the water as an example of this adolescent fascination with the unknowable. "The mysterioso thing," Wolfe has them thinking, "was how [Simmons] could have died at all. If he had been one of the old pan-thuhs [i.e., ridiculed adults], hell, sure he could have got killed. But Simmons was, well, one's own age, he was the kind of guy who could have been in the Pump House gang, he was . . . *immune*, he was plugged into the whole pattern, he could feel the whole Oh Mighty Hulking Sea, he didn't have to think it out step by step. But he got wiped out and killed. Very mysterioso."

Leave aside the fact that Simmons's real handicap was a bad arm and not, as Wolfe reports, a bad leg; forget that Wolfe's "Simmons boy" was not only *not* "one's own age" but was thirty-five years old when he died—in Wolfe's terms, a panther himself. Ignore that Wolfe appears not to know who Simmons was or that he had died fourteen years before Wolfe's writing. Wolfe's real error comes in reading the gang's wonderment as vanity: legendary surfer Robert Simmons, living for years in his car and surfing up and down the state, most assuredly *was* plugged into the whole pattern and certainly *didn't* have to think it all out step-by-step. That's not mysticism, it's water knowledge gained over a lifetime. And to say that a panther—a middle-aged tourist from a land-locked state—would be more likely to die in giant surf than a man who'd devoted his life to understanding it is neither ageism nor xenophobia, it's just common sense. Wolfe ought to have known that one learns little about baseball in a locker-room interview; why not allow that surfers, like so many of us, could be inarticulate about the most important thing in their lives? Had he no curiosity about what they actually did in the water? No compunction to describe even one of them riding a wave? C. R. Stecyk writes in *The Surfer's Journal* that Wolfe, on his Easterner's quest for western material, went first to Malibu. A sensible place to get the scoop on surfing—those Gidget and beach-party movies having already made Malibu world-famous. But as the white-suited New Yorker walked down to "the pit," he was "welcomed in the way all outsiders were," Stecyk writes. "He was summarily pelted with pebbles, bottles and human excrement." Deplorable behavior, to be sure, but it explains Wolfe's grudge against ageism, the fury of the ultimate insider at his own irrelevance; one wonders why Wolfe didn't tell us about it himself.

It's worth adding, however, that Wolfe missed material that would've suited his purpose beautifully. If he'd stuck around Malibu a little longer, he could've met its undisputed king and the éminence grise of 1960s surfing: Mickey "Da Cat" Dora. To this day, though Dora no longer lives in the United States, "Da Cat" still appears spray-painted on the seawall at Malibu, apparently reappears upon being covered over. Mike Doyle remembers Dora as having "such charisma and style," and legendary big-wave surfer Greg Noll remembers him as "a tremendous athlete who surfed with a beautiful, smooth, natural style." Dora's feline smoothness and grace in the Malibu crowds are impossible to miss in the old films. He's one of those guys who, for better or worse, oozes cool. A wine importer's son schooled in military academies, Dora loved to generate mystique—hinting that his stepfather, who died boating, had been murdered, and insisting that JFK's assassination had cursed California's best breaks with smaller waves. Dora acquired much of his notoriety by playing the purist about the commercialization of surfing. Writing for *The Surfer's Journal* (published as fiction but sworn by Noll in editorial notes to be true), Bruce Savage remembers taking Dora to see Noll's *Search for Surf*. When the film started, Dora noticed a very pregnant woman in front of him, and Dora took out a 35mm thunder cracker, put it under the woman's seat, and lit the fuse. Savage writes that just after Dora slipped out the door, the woman was blown into the aisle, where she twisted in agony as her husband screamed and wept. Regardless of the story's truth, it feeds the Dora legend.

But in spite of this, and in spite of Dora's actually appearing in Hollywood rip-offs like *Gidget Goes to Rome* and *Ride the Wild Surf* (in which his stunt work is quite impressive, surfing big North Shore effortlessly on his first island visit), Greg Noll still sees him as "one of the few guys that honestly believes in his soul, that when he endorses something he's giving up a part of himself." Noll was, of course, the one guy who managed to market Dora's pretense to purity, with the Greg Noll Surfboards Mickey Dora model, called "Da Cat" (recently the subject of a counterfeiting operation). One of the advertisements—with no hint of irony—depicted Dora on a garbage can, throwing away his Duke Kahanamoku 1966 contest trophy. "Scrap metal tokenism as a grubby little payoff," the product advertisement read, "to keep me in line and my mouth shut. Such outside pressures will never succeed in making me a lapdog for the entrenched controlling interests who have turned our once great individualistic sport into a mushy, soggy cartoon." Another of the ads smacks of Nietzschean disdain for the common man. "I don't want some acne-stricken adolescent in Pratt Falls, Iowa," it read, "using Da Cat for a car ornament or some show-biz creep in the Malibu Colony using Da Cat as a coffee table. Da Cat is too pure and sensitive for the clumsy touch of the occasional pseudo surfer." A third put Dora at the top of the evolutionary scale, genetically superior to lesser surfers in recognizably fascist terms. Something about this strikes at the heart of surfer loathing for the larger world and its corrupting pursuits, just the kind of xenophobia I'd enjoyed while driving around listening to Vince rail against the Barneys from over the hill, car-phoning their surf observations to software-engineer friends, or against all the Johnnies-come-lately thinking they have any right to surf the Point (somehow, my own status had still never come up). Such sentiments may just reveal the usual human competitiveness, but they also seem related to the price any dedicated surfer has paid. So much devotion for so little material gain or status makes any presumption by the uncommitted a cheapening of all that lost time.

In *Surfers, the Movie*, Dora explains his distaste for modern life: "I can't live in the northern hemisphere," he says, "I must live back, back into time where all these animals, all this life, the oysters, the shellfish, everything, all is part of this smell, everything is part of this focus . . . The whole magnificence of riding waves is that living being, that communication between you and the whole existence of reality on this planet." The link between nature's purity and xenophobia is apparent in Dora's other great claim to fame: as the archetypal Surf Nazi. Surfers had played with the trappings of Nazism for years—in the 1930s, The Swastika Surfboard Company, a subsidiary of Pacific System Homes, promoted its swastika-emblazoned boards with social-realist advertising, and in 1959, C. R. Stecyk reports in *The Surfer's Journal*, United States surfing champion Jack Haley and a retinue of uniformed Wehrmacht storm troopers goose-stepped barefoot into the Point Loma Theater, sat down, lit farts in unison, and shouted "Sieg heil." Stecyk explains the surfer craze for Nazi uniforms as harmless play with stuff everyone's father brought back from the war—swords, helmets, Nazi officer's uniforms—and Noll sees Dora's painting swastikas on surfboards in the same light: he knew it pissed people off, so he did it. Certainly, this makes some sense, given that the perpetrators were mostly kids with little knowledge of the Holocaust (the same excuse could be given, of course, for today's skinheads). But Mike Doyle also remembers Dora showing up to play tennis in Beverly Hills—a very Jewish town—wearing a full-length trench coat covered with Nazi war medals, a Nazi cap, and a swastika on a chain around his neck. And even Dora's scheme to burn down the San Onofre beach shack and paint swastikas on the outhouses—pitting surf Nazism against island style—opposed white pride to the "native" side of the surfing aesthetic. Doyle writes that in 1973 Dora got busted passing bad checks, skipped probation, and disappeared; that years later Dora was arrested in Biarritz and spent a few months in French jails before being deported. (Some time before that, Vince met him in a surfer's squatter home in Spain, again in the Canary Islands—remembers not caring much for the guy.) After serving his jail time in the States, Dora apparently moved to South Africa (of all places). Much later, interviewed for *Surfers, the Movie*, Dora sums it all up: "My whole life is this escape, my whole life is this wave I drop into . . . and shoot for my life, going for broke, man, and behind me, all the shit goes over my back . . . the screaming parents . . . screaming teachers, police, priests, politicians, kneeboarders, windsurfers . . . they're all going over the falls head first . . . into the fucking reef . . . Buow! And I'm shooting for my life and when it starts to close out I pull off the bottom out to the back and I pick off another one and do the same goddamn thing."

21

Winter's end comes slowly, as the days lengthen and the swells shorten, and you wonder when the dreaded northwesterlies will start blowing onshore in the afternoons, ruining the surf from the vernal equinox in March through the autumnal equinox in September. On a late February day with the grasses lush green but not yet whipped dry for summer, I called my uncle on the phone, told him that theory of mine about surfing not being a story. I hadn't seen him since a climbing trip the previous summer, but we talked from time to time, compared swell notes. I've never heard anyone describe the shapes and behavior of waves with more effortless precision than Jim, and although he has a steel-trap mind for facts, his wave knowledge is all experiential.

"Nah," Jim responded to my theory, "that's not really true. I mean, the story's really the whole grail quest."

"Like the Holy Grail?"

"You know, you wake up one morning hung over from all the mescal you swilled in some Ensenada shit-hole, you're like, wondering *why* you had to eat that second worm, and then . . . you know, you remember this really weird dream you had the night before. Yeah, about some grizzled old loony at the bar, right? This half-crazy dude rambling about perfect, empty waves at some mysto secret spot way the hell down in deepest Baja." He cleared his throat and I grabbed a pen. "In your dream—Wasn't it a dream? you ask—the grizzled dude grabbed a napkin and some stub of a pencil and started making all these chicken scratches, you know, about two hundred miles on some dirt road, maybe turn left at the bent cactus, blah-blah-blah, and then when you roll out of bed to look for some aspirin you see, on the floor, the *napkin*!" He paused while we both laughed, and then he added, "So, you start driving that morning, and after a great journey, maybe you score perfect waves, or"—his voice took on a mock-mystical groove—"maybe you find something you weren't even looking for."

The other plot, of course, is the big-wave plot, the one I'd started with myself. For years, I'd looked at pictures of big waves and imagined they were just giant versions of the benign smaller waves I'd ridden—same mellow fun, just more of it. Wrong, of course, and if the search for good surf is the Quest for the Grail, then the big-wave story is that of the Dragon Slayer. Forgetting the endless summer, ignoring perpetual youth, the Dragon Slayer telescopes everything into one momentous test, a linear tale with an inescapable conclusion. No surfer lived closer to that myth than Greg Noll whom, in Noll's delightful biography, *Da Bull, Life over the Edge*, Fred Hemmings describes as "a modern-day mountain man like the legendary characters of the Rockies during the days of the Wild West . . . Not the kind of guy you would find eating quiche." Noll remembers feeling that "there wasn't a wave that God could produce that I couldn't ride. I visualized men going into battle in the days of King Arthur, not knowing if they would live or die, but feeling supremely confident and alive . . ." Ken Bradshaw, a world-famous present-day big-wave rider, remarks, "I come from the same school of thought that Greg does. I believe that surfing should be done exactly as it was meant to be done: man *versus* the ocean" (my italics). The huge wave Noll rode at Makaha in 1969 stands to this day as the fulfillment of the archetype, the ultimate fish story. Already legendary as a big-wave surfer, board shaper, and all-around wild man, Noll had been living in southern California, running a very successful surfboard company and surf shop and producing surf films; he had flown to Oahu just for this swell, one big enough to produce the rare and fabled big Makaha Point surf. "The water was nearly as smooth as glass," Noll remembers, ". . . and the waves were so big that they literally put the fear of God in me"—fifty feet at the outside point. Police were barricading the road and evacuating homes.

"Deep down inside," Noll writes, "I had always wanted to ride a bigger wave than anyone else had ever ridden. Now here was my chance. After a lifetime of working up to it," he explains with characteristic bluntness, "the time had finally come to either shit or get off the pot." Outside at the lineup, he remembers beads of water dancing on his board from wave impacts a quarter mile away, breaking lips taking three seconds to touch down. Of the wave that finally comes for him, Noll says, "You could have stacked two eighteen-wheel semis on top of each other against the face . . . and still have had room left over to ride it." He makes the long, long drop—all he hoped to do—and then a section "a block and a half long" starts to break. The wave "threw out a sheet of water over my head and engulfed me," Noll remembers. "Then for a split second the whole scene froze forever in my mind. There I was in that liquid green room . . . I had been in and out of this room many times. Only this time the room was bigger, more frightening, with the thunderous roar of the ocean bouncing off its walls. I realized I wasn't going to go flying out the other end into daylight." Hemmings calls it a "death wish wave," and says that "if it had been anyone else . . . he would have died." And when Noll finally swims to shore, amazingly unhurt, his friend Buffalo hands him a beer and says, "Good ting you wen make 'em, brudda, 'cause no way I was comin' in afta you. I was jus goin' wave goodbye and say 'Alooo-ha.' " As is fitting, with the dragon slain, Noll stops surfing, testament both to his relationship to water and to his knowledge of self: he did what he'd set out to do, then moved on.

Twenty-five years after Noll, Oahu-based Mark Foo replicated that quest, but in the other direction. A professional surfer, television sportscaster, and surfing journalist who had built his career riding the world's biggest surf, Foo bought an open-ended Honolulu–San Francisco airline ticket in order to be ready for a great swell at Mavericks, a big-wave break between Santa Cruz and San Francisco. He finally tracked the right storm across the Pacific, flew in overnight, and by noon was dead. His body floated for almost an hour before it was found at the breakwater near the harbor entrance. According to Jenkins, Foo "had given up everything, including a relationship with his parents, to pursue a single-minded assault on big waves." His sister remarked to a journalist, "Surfing is not what good Chinese boys do. They go to school, become doctors and lawyers. But Mark was at peace with himself. Many times he told me he was going to die young, and this is how he wanted to go." He was sucked back up over the falls after a wipeout, and had a cut on his head—probably from his board, which was broken into at least three pieces. But Foo appears to have died by drowning, perhaps tied to the reef by his own leash. Ocean Beach's Doc Renneker examined the body: "He was laying in the back of the boat," Renneker told the papers, "with his wetsuit pulled down off his chest. I stood there looking at him. His musculature was perfect. He was in perfect condition. He looked like the fallen hero." But really, it wasn't a great drama. It was actually a smallish day at Mavericks, much smaller than waves Foo had ridden hundreds of times at Waimea Bay. Foo had told a Hawaiian newspaper columnist in 1989, "For some reason, when it's really big, I'm most at peace with myself. Even though you're intimidated, you have to leave fear behind and accept the possibility of dying." Such is the fickleness of fate: Noll rode a true death wave and lived, while Foo, who had ridden many such waves beautifully, died on a smaller one. It prompts our compulsive Icarus stories, but doesn't finally fit the myth.

Mavericks, California's only true "big wave" break, actually broke that year on a morning I happened to be passing by. A place where very deep water shoaled quickly enough for open ocean swell to break at tremendous sizes, Mavericks only broke a few times each year, some years not at all. For more than a decade, a local named Jeff Clark had surfed it more or less alone, but in the last few years it had acquired international status on a par with the great breaks at Oahu's Waimea Bay and Baja's Todos Santos. I'd been in Berkeley for the weekend, visiting Susan, and on the elevated freeway west, I heard small-craft radio advisories, high-surf warnings for the State Beaches. South of San Francisco, the highway left squalid suburbs for thousand-foot bluffs and greenhouses of flowers, bristling artichoke fields windrowed with gnarled cypress trees, and below crumbling artillery platforms, guano-smeared fins of stone took the biggest swell I'd ever seen. Because breaking waves express the benthic topography, giant surf reveals deep water contours otherwise only mythic; as I drove, big blue walls crashed over reefs I'd never imagined. I slowed down to watch, let car after car pass angrily by. My tape deck had been eviscerating cassettes lately, so when radio reception failed, no choice but quiet anticipation. Three million people just behind that coastal range, yet an illusion of great remove: two lanes of asphalt separating clean dunes from a glassy lagoon, a woman in a blue jacket standing in the reeds watching water birds drift while a hundred yards away foam boomed and sprayed. Driving among drivers to whom this magical swell didn't (and shouldn't) mean anything. Around a bluff, a big black harrier hawk sat folded up on a fence post: bullet-shaped, thick-chested, hook-beaked. And although the highway lay across that continental edge like a corridor of accelerated time, every mile or two perched another raptor on a fence post or power line awaiting the day's warmth—all evenly spaced, giving each other room in their timeless, gory lives.

A white-picketed clapboard compound called Ocean View Farms sat among gargantuan, sprawling Monterey pines—nothing rustling or breezy about those firm, mountainlike trees—and hippie enclaves of shingled, organically shaped shacks clustered near the old shipyards at Pillar Point, offshore of which lay Mavericks. The dirt parking lot overflowed with cars and ten-foot boards: rhino chasers, elephant guns (named after the oversized weaponry used in big-game hunting). When a wave's face gets to be twenty-five or thirty feet high, the volume of water rushing up its face makes paddling downward very difficult. Thus the size of the boards, allowing a surfer to overcome the surface friction, to reach a paddling speed close enough to the wave's speed. Very different from classic rounded longboards, guns come to stiletto points at nose and tail and often have inch-thick wooden stringers for reinforcement. They also have a great quality of seriousness about them; just owning one indicates a certain intent. Something that would lurk in your closet year-round, reminding you of a fight you'd picked but hadn't fought. And in the dirt stood a focused older crowd among their pickups and vans, waxing boards, stuffing wetsuits into backpacks. Most wearing hats and sunglasses, not talking much.

I walked out a path to the point, then scrambled up a footworn and eroding slope to a big air-force installation with three satellite/radar dishes and chain-link fence topped with barbed wire. (Radar apparently there to track incoming intercontinental ballistic missiles—warlike, grave military men inside; warlike, grave athletes outside.) Along the cliff, in ice-plant green from one angle and iridescent red from another, an audience of twenty or thirty gazed out at the ten or fifteen surfers—black dots rising and falling, easily mistaken for a cluster of diving birds. Mostly men watching, but a few women; several video cameras, one film camera. Not much conversation—surfers aren't generally jovial and gregarious among strangers, have too much at stake, wouldn't want to be overheard saying anything stupid. Two broken boards lay on the mud flat, and a surfer walked aimlessly and dazed in the tidal shallows with his wetsuit around his waist. He appeared delirious as he pushed through the brackish murk and dragged his fingertips along the surface. A blimp advertising cinnamon liqueur circled the lineup as two photographer's boats waited in the deep-water channel to the south. A man in baggy pants and hooded sweatshirt told me a teenager had just gone down with the lip of a twenty-five-foot wave; he'd free-fallen the whole way, broken the board, come in for another, and paddled back out. There's an odd mixture of drama and anticlimax in watching such a scene; I stood safe on a windless bluff while those dots nearly a mile off barely moved. Without the surfers as yardsticks, I would never have realized how large the waves were. Many were thirty feet from trough to lip, a few seemed bigger, and all were on a different order of magnitude from the waves in which I had nearly drowned. But now and then one of these blackish-green ramparts would surge through the crowd of hopefuls, someone would get his board up to speed, hit his feet, and drop; and occasionally get thrown into space by the lip, as though he'd leapt off a three-story building (one that happened to be going twenty-five knots). Jeff Clark has said that when you wipe out, Mavericks holds you under water like you owe it money; it did seem that an unlucky few were out of the picture for a long time, being driven onto a reef below thirty feet of cold, black water. But from so far off, the danger, speed, and power were hard to feel.

But then I noticed a disturbance a half mile outside the clustered surfers, a place where the sea itself seemed to have a divot or wrinkle, an inexplicable cant in the very angle of the ocean surface. The surfers scrambled for safety, and when that phase shift caught the deeply submerged chunk of reef, it stood up in a vast, dark-green cathedral wall. Ten-foot boards looked like tiny splinters as they rose to the wave's shaking lip—the whole thing just lifting and lifting, perhaps forty to forty-five vertical feet above those men caught in the trough. But one lay still on his board, barely paddling as the wave drew him up its face—confident in his place in the curve. Just as the wall sucked concave, its Promethean reach complete, the man crested the wave and sat up on his board. Not to surf, but to watch its lip soar forward with stately deadliness of purpose, clear past the sloping wall. A half mile away, where I stood with hat on amid a cloud of white noise softening all sonic edges, the lip's impact sounded clear and hard like a concussion I'd once heard in the High Sierra in the silence of night, a guttural boom as a whole piece of mountain detonated against some remote valley floor.

That one man's backward glance, the sanguine curiosity required to peer into such an abyss, struck me as a characteristic response to such power—like the mountaineer who, facing a great icefall, is struck first by its beauty, only later by its worthiness as an adversary. And whatever spirit it took, Mark Foo shared. "I paddled over a solid twenty-five-foot wave," Foo remembers in Drew Kampion's *The Book of Waves*, ". . . and I saw this thing, . . . the biggest thing I'd ever seen." Thing, not wave: it had, for him, transcended sport—even water. Of the fifty-foot wave he dove deep under and survived, Foo recalls, "The funny thing is, I think I laughed . . . it was so unbelievable. It was like a cartoon almost." Perhaps this is the meaning outside plots and stories: the meaning made by bald wonder. John Severson—as quoted by Drew Kampion—recalls a giant day at Oahu's Makaha, taking off on a twenty-five-foot wave and getting caught behind the big Makaha bowl. Swept over the falls, he gets drilled thirty feet through the water to the bottom, and as the wave holds him there, he thinks through his whole life, says goodbye to his loved ones, realizes that, "I was paying for high adventure with my life. But it seemed like a fair trade." But like Foo's, his memory of the wave itself is far different, and utterly without bravado: as he soars toward what he calls "the big tamale" (death), he has a sudden moment of clarity when he sees the lip leaping out into space. "Wow, this is beautiful and awesome," he remembers thinking, ". . . sun reflections bouncing off the glassy blue surface . . ."

George Downing, also in *The Book of Waves*, has a similar memory from that day: noticing "way on the western horizon toward Kaena Point, a very unusual, black shadow. At first I thought it was a trick of light, of sun and cloud, then I realized it was a set of waves." He starts drifting outside his lineup (in this case, a triangulation of points on land that tells a surfer where he is over the shoaling reef), then farther out, thinking he's in such deep water that waves couldn't possibly break there. Two hundred yards outside, he paddles over four waves in a row, each bigger than the previous one, all of which he describes as the biggest he's ever seen. When he crosses the fourth, he remembers, "In front of me was a wave bigger than all the others. It was already starting to curl over at the top, far above me. Its face was sheer and pock-marked with boils caused by its suction on the reef far below. I had been paddling for a while now, but it was not fatigue that made me stop. It was something else that's hard to put into words. I was coming up out of that awful trough, starting up the face, when I looked over to my right, toward the Point, where this most incredible wave was already breaking, pitching out a lip so thick and powerful it was beyond my comprehension. And the space that it framed, that enormous tube, was so massive, on such a different scale from anything I'd ever seen, that it was just too much. Then I realized that the wave was actually sucking me up the face. I pushed my board away and dove for the bottom."

Eventually, I turned southward, thinking I might look again at big waves hitting the Point—see with different eyes the scene in which I'd been so stupid two years before. Where the Mavericks road rejoined the highway, fishermen camped in RVs at crappy roadside sites near a one-room schoolhouse. Back in traffic, the world rushing along as the great punctuation of one tale became again an irrelevancy in every other. The Nurserymen's Exchange and its greenhouses of seedlings, bulbs—American flags waved toward the sea in the clear offshore breeze. And then my radio picked up this free-floating trace of noise, a little fragment from across the hills producing a woman's voice on a talk show, outraged about toxins in food and their responsibility for various cancers. Just as she faded out, a hawk tilted in the wind, traced the scurryings of a mouse down in the cattle-cropped shortgrass; just being there and doing it, time after time, day after day, circling, hovering, fluttering, soaring, striking. South of Half Moon Bay, the sun lit up the white roofs of the Coastside Lutheran and Baptist churches and a lone white house stood far across artichoke fields, stark against cattle-range hills. Piled pallets rotted among rusted old trucks. A forlorn-looking man walked along the open highway, not hitchhiking and never looking up (resigned to the disinterestedness of mankind? An impractical misanthrope?). At another field of mustard, acres of yellow floated by the sea among buckskin-brown grass. Where the road curved along very high cliffs, a bouquet of calla lilies and wilting wildflowers hung from a rusted iron post by the brink—offerings, perhaps, to someone who'd taken a last look from here. Wide Pescadero Creek meandered out of its broad valley, and a few half-drowned, half-dried trees lay uprooted in the mud as surging foam rushed among the tide pools. For miles, the road dropped to beaches where creeks drained to the sea, rose along cliffs and curved around hills of new grass. At Bean Hollow, a slender marsh hawk hunted low over new foxtails as primary colors stole the spectrum: oxalis sprinkled yellow among the million fingers of the scallion crop, all waving by a bright-blue and whitecapping sea. A produce stand sold white corn, peas, strawberries, artichokes. Then suddenly I could see past Año Nuevo Island (where herds of sea lions—culled by white sharks—inhabited an abandoned lighthouse), clear across the bay to where the indistinct silhouette of the Santa Lucias seemed the very essence of *mountain*. Migrant workers in yellow slickers packed green onions near a ranch where my mother rode horses as a teenage camp counselor. (She remembers eating strawberries in the sunshine one afternoon when a farmer's son offered to take her flying in his little Cessna. They'd dive-bombed coves and soared over beaches, and she always told the story as a confession, bewildered by the sensuous good luck of a California childhood.)

At a downgrade beneath eroding sandstone cliffs, I crossed a flooding creek (the swell utterly overwhelming the beach) where a bear once ripped apart an early rancher. Elk and antelope and packs of wolves once wandered this range; ten-foot grizzlies fed on hundred-foot beached whales. The mountains steepened at a lumber yard where thirty years of surfer lookouts had etched sandy paths through the succulents—an obscure patch of earth intimately known. And Davenport, a little clapboard and Victorian village: store, school, two coffee shops; in my mother's memory, blanketed with white dust from the local concrete plant. The stark white Presbyterian church still faced west, still watched whales pass from Arctic summers to Baja winters. Just south, near the former site of an Ohlone Indian village, two surfers stood on a railway berm looking passively at the violent sea. (The village's shell mound, 270 feet long, ninety feet wide and twenty feet high, was said to hold mussel shells, gumboot chiton plates, black turban snails, red abalone, purple sea urchin tines, bits of chipped flint and obsidian, boiling stones: ten thousand years of detritus.) I stopped nearby, stepped over broken auto glass, climbed the hand-and-foot-polished branches of a cypress near the Point: past the lagoon patrolled by that local white marsh hawk, obscenely out-scaled walls surged across the cove, boomed off the cliffs, and sent spray thirty and forty feet in the air. I looked at the road I'd gone running blindly down and the beach where I'd washed ashore, now as much a part of my life as anyone's sidewalk. And that near disaster seemed meaningless, just a recreational failure of judgment; the triumph, if any, lay in having been here enough to feel at home. My eye followed instead the bird: I realized I'd never seen him or any raptor out over the water. They'd trace the cliff brush but never so much as loop a little over the sea, and I didn't blame them. At all.

Spring

Call me Queequeg . . .

THOMAS FARBER
On Water

22

Spring happens—one day you look out, and that first drizzly, foggy morning, a sure sign of seasonal change, has turned to northwesterly winds roughening a waveless ocean into shining whitecaps. For the next few months, you keep mornings free and resign yourself to blown-out, unsurfable afternoons; prepare for the even greater misery of summer, when the ocean can sit dead flat for weeks at a time between southern hemisphere pulses. The morning fog drawn ashore by inland heat breaks up in vague and varied depths; visibility comes in leaps and starts as headlands tear off shreds of cloud. When the mist retreats, the mother bank rolls thick along the horizon and the wind blows down like a transparent cloud itself, a broad arc of dark-blue motion pressing south along the paler field of stillness. The whitecaps then seem to sprint together as if the sun had tipped their jar and spilled them all at once; one often sees them coming, sits in the glassy cove watching the ripped-up outer waters, knowing one's session will soon end. Ocean much, much colder than in winter—those winds blow off the surface and churn up frigid bottom water even as they draw precious moisture and life out of the grasses and flowers, bring on the long dead time of summer. And standing on the cliff watching all that change, I thought how much we let views tell us the kind of world we live in: at that moment, a fading lush one of running grain and blossoms, sparrow chirps nearly lost in air that just that morning had cycled through far-northern lungs. The hawk soared in sharp, bolting upwind flights over a fallow field, the field itself a grid with a message. If culture is the mess of ideas and feelings through which we read the world, it also responds to that world's particularity: certainly I had well-formed notions and terms for exalted response to place, but certainly also this given place picked from among them. We aren't entirely trapped in the prison house of language, and an urban grid reflects back ourselves quite differently than does this coast; the hawk makes a unique argument about what constitutes a well-lived life. The waving fields—like those in which prairie settlers saw the motions of the sea—and even the tractor's wheel dust and chimney exhaust slashing south in that pale sky tell something particular about time and scale. That wind, after all, doesn't blow through the sky; it *is* the sky, moving as a whole over the furrow.

But in the port city of Kiel, on the north coast of Germany, Mitch and Thore knew nothing about northern Californian surf seasons or wind patterns: they'd plotted for three years to blow out of the Old World for some New World fun, and weren't going to let trivial details stop them. Thore, a sail maker just out of high school, practiced surfing in locally generated wind chop and sent copies of *Surfer* to Mitch in the army. Circled photos of juicy tube rides, islander girls in thong bikinis, destinations for their pilgrimage: Rincon, Malibu, Steamer Lane. Mitch's service delayed things, but then suddenly he was out. They'd fly to San Francisco, hitchhike to Santa Cruz to buy boards and a VW van, then surf and camp their way to Costa Rica. A waiter at a Kiel restaurant, a hard-core North Sea surfer named Frank, had met some great Californians in Santa Cruz and still had the address, had been happy to pass it along. Now, after two days of travel, they were on my couch.

"Ve here from Frank," said Thore, broad-shouldered and boyish with an eager face and natty blond hair. With his mouth shut, he could easily have been a pro surfer, had clearly studied the part. Mitch, bald and built like a wrestler, seemed more ashamed than Thore at their imposition and knew little English. Thore knew even less, but it didn't stop him: "To surf," he said, "is okay to stay?"

Stunning, but I—of all people—could sympathize, even if I'd never heard of either Frank or the guy he'd stayed with. After all, it *was* a great vision: two buddies clear across the world, drifting through the outback, sleeping by fires on beaches, meeting California girls, smoking weed, and surfing their Deutsche brains out. Then lolling about in a tropical paradise for a year. Sure, Thore had fallen fiercely, dependently in love one month before their flight, but she'd agreed to meet them in Costa Rica—a beauty at the end of the rainbow. We had a great time surfboard shopping, and once again I got to be the local who knew everything, the kahuna: I had the pleasure of translating all the arcane details about board shape, and the surf-shop employees were knocked out by the boldness of the quest. It immediately marked the foreigners as great guys, confirmed that we're all just Americans at heart. "Classic," the locals drawled, when they'd heard the plan. And the boys went nuts in the shops, temples to a life that had seemed as ethereal and impossible as Hollywood itself: original balsa boards on the walls, radical new designs, outrageous action videos, and, best of all, real surfers buying the boards, wearing the clothes, talking the talk. We picked out some beauties and the guys took all the decals the shops could spare.

Our first session up at the Point turned out to be Mitch's first ever: he paddled out, went over the falls on one of the rare healthy-sized waves, got clobbered, and called it a day; shivered on the cliff while Thore and I thrashed at wind-whipped little rills. Inconsistent and awfully cold—no sunbathers in sight—it wasn't quite what Thore had imagined either. The guys in the water asked about surfing in Germany, but Thore's English wasn't good enough for more than, Yes, there were waves. On our walk back to the truck, I noticed the morning's tightly rolled poppies had opened to flutter in the wind. Even the light that evening was different, a spring but not summer sunset, the first long twilight with a pollinated vibrance as dusk pinks finally lingered before dark. But something about the cold water got the boys looking aggressively at buses; in a peculiar show of nationalism, they would consider only Volkswagens. Two whole days on our porch, hoping for the dream car: a tidy, serviceable engine, double bed, fridge, and stove. But bus after bus went away unwanted: Costa Rica was a long ways off and fifteen hundred dollars didn't buy reliability. So one day, spirits low and the household tired of their dirty dishes, the Germans walked into the kitchen with airline tickets to Costa Rica. Santa Cruz hadn't turned out to be a full-time carnival anyway; just a place people lived, a tawdry little town in the middle of a flat spell. And suddenly, there was hope: El Dorado might still be out there. The day after they left, the surf came up and I walked out to the Point, thinking how as a traveler, money spent and time off taken, one could end up just drinking in a crummy cantina or hiding from the rain at a Fosters Freeze. But these guys had what you'd call stoke; I pictured them thrashing their flat, frigid hometown water (a harbor my grandfather's B-17 had bombed in World War II), dreaming of California, maybe having a cup of coffee afterwards, reading a *Surfer* news flash to the effect of "Brock and Laird Score Perfect Easter Island Barrels!"

It was a misty spring dawn, fog thick and poppies rolled back up tight, and the entire goddamn sprout field—the whole hundred acres—screamed a now-hallucinogenic yellow under the low clouds, and on the beach little sea stars and sea peas shone in the sand while ice plant bloomed with violet daisies. Ruler-edged waves peeled through the still, fog-glassed sea. And the hills were so green with new grass and foxtails that the oxalis was no longer the lone flag of color; fresh, leafy hemlock shoots filled in among the old dead ones, grew well overhead and waved in the breeze like more wild wheat. I thought again about throwing language all over a scene, wondered if the emotional mystery of one's response to place doesn't lie in the inchoate play of *possible* words, of felt meanings and poetries, of the sublime, the romantic, the picturesque, Zen; even, perhaps, something new. And perhaps that twinge of disappointment one always feels at the words chosen—and thus also at the glorious scene—comes from the dream that in that instant of indecision and all-decision before your mind clarified its response to beauty, you just might have held within you language finally saturated with all the earth's meaning.

Heading for the water early to beat the winds, to play in small waves just for dermal salination therapy: the point being, I now know for certain, not at all the thrill of risk or the pride of achievement, but rather the dailiness of well-spent time, the accumulation of moments that will never translate into anything but a private sense of well-being. And, willy-nilly, surfing had made a dedicated birder of me—I suppose mostly because one sat for so long between waves these days, the winter swells gone, summer souths not yet here. One floated idle, watched whatever was there to be watched; took particular interest in all forms of soaring. Perhaps also because birds swim through the air as much as fly, demonstrate that we live in an ether—not a vacuum—don't finally face the voids we imagine. I'd never cared about birds before this year, had always found the idea of birding tedious. I still feel no affinity for songbirds, though I imagine there will come a time when their inoffensive cheeriness and light living will seem an appropriate ideal. Although still working hard and climbing on weekends, my father says it already seems one to him. On Sunday afternoons, he takes a secular Sabbath there in Berkeley's flatlands, receives no visitors, and sits in a folding chair in the unmown grass practicing a new obsession: flamenco guitar. Complex finger patterns, Spanish drama and passion—all the while watching (with the musician's abstracted stare) the hoarding of the local squirrel. And he swears that on evenings warm enough for him to drink wine out there with Mom, all the local sparrows gather on the power lines as the sun sets—not a single eye facing east. A good view, too, I'd imagine, past a giant Monterey pine in a neighbor's yard, across the descending alluvial plain of Berkeley's warehouse district, over the bay to the mystical mountain form of Tamalpais—a black plate lain over the color of the falling night.

As I walked alone down the road, there in the din of the sea was the local harrier, the marsh hawk, yet again hunting the bulrushes and arroyo willows of the little gulch, solitary soarer among societies of scavenging gulls and diving, amorous auks. For hours, days, years, a lifetime: down the hill, over the reeds, up the mustard of the other side, then low again over the minilagoon—tending his fields. I often wondered if he ever just forgot his prey and went on banking these hills for sheer pleasure. I lay for an hour before getting wet, let the fog break up, and watched a kestrel kite on a draft pushing up the sandstone cliffs—a tiny falconiforme, also surfing morning thermal bubbles too cool and weak for the bigger buzzard hawks. Riding a few feet over the hemlock, eyes glaring into drying foxtails the wheat color of gold. Body frozen, loose, thin wings spread like fluttering fingers, tips up in a slight V; rusty-red tail wide and talons clawing open. Poised on the push from marine to continental, focused on a shrew, a little snake, perhaps a field mouse to swallow whole. Its hooked, flesh-tearing beak so different from the plucking tools of the shorebirds. Then the kestrel stopped flapping, froze its wings and spread its tail, and fell down through the air cushion, parachuting onto its prey. It dropped several times without luck, then banked before the sun; its feathers shone for an instant as an X-rayed fan of backlit bone and fiber. Then it pulled flat and soared on no apparent breeze, along a strip of wilderness between fields. It perched finally on a yellow lupine, and its turretlike head surveyed, rotated: land bird hunting in land's last ecology.

And a family of shorebirds, back from winter wanderings, were home again at the Point and had taken up residence in the cliff: spring breeding. Black with red feet, white patches on their backs, thick torpedo bodies: pigeon guillemots pairing off and building nests on little broken ledges where their eggs would be safe from crows, then bobbing along as a group in the swell. Strength in numbers, so irresistibly tribal. Diving for fish, these odd little birds *fly* underwater, propelled by their wings rather than their feet, and the adaptation has its costs: their short, sharp wings work madly to keep those thick bodies aloft. Sprinklers shot up from hundred-yard pipes and farm workers took orders from the farmer; no surfers in the water. Ended up alone among reddish-brown patches of kelp with a roar in my ears from surf and no talk. A black pelagic cormorant with white flank patches flapped in hard and steady, just off the waves but not air surfing. It backpedaled suddenly and came to a stop, bent over and stuck its neck under to look for bottom dwellers, crab and eel; its water-adapted retinas and lenses seeing so much more than my eyes would. And then it plopped over and dove; up again a moment later, a rockfish impaled on the little hook of its upper beak. For over two thousand years, Chinese fishermen have trained these slender black birds to forage. Reared in captivity and raised on tofu, the wing-clipped cormorants respond to spoken and whistled commands; neck rings keep them from swallowing the catch, but after seven fish, the rings come off and they fish for themselves. Once they've caught the seventh, one reads, they refuse to dive until the band is loosened—cormorants can count.

I dropped in and slid out in the foam along a wave's base; off balance, I lost speed, and the suck of water up the wave's face took me with it. Misplaced in the energy curve, I caught the tangled curl across my chest and got thrown down and cartwheeled with my board between my legs. Dragged backwards, held under, released. Popped up amid floating fluff that marked the impact zone. Lingering bubbles hung deep through the water like broken white capillaries aerating the reef dwellers, fluffing the otter's fur. Above, tentacles of foam marbled the pale-green water, bubbling and hissing; I inhaled a wisp and coughed. Floated with the wetsuit's buoyancy and watched the end of the Point: cliff swallows huddled in little mud caves molded into cliff crannies under loose blocks, a city for a season on a fast-eroding precipice. Nobody needs to be told that spring's all about sex, but it's still a treat to see it at a place you've watched all winter: like a cloud of insects the cliff swallows shot back from the wall, swirled out over the tidal flat to dodge and fight, then as a body flocked back. They flapped against each other and thrashed into their little cliff dwellings, played musical nests. Then, as one pulled headfirst into a hole, another mounted it from behind and they fell. Locked in static intercourse they never flapped, so their four open wings made an organic helicopter and the mating pair swirled down over jagged sandstone boulders, parting only a few feet above. Then they sprinted back into the cloud of frantic, sex-crazed birds, male chasing female, dodging among their extended clan. Soon, she took them out of the group and high over the draining mid-littoral sea grass; they feinted and dodged, banked off each other and shot apart. Then, trajectories and intentions at last in sync, they locked bodies a hundred feet above exposed reef. Again—the helicopter, rotating as they slipped through the air; down, and down, and when once again the time came to part and rejoin the swarm, they chose not to. Too late to pull the cord, the lovers smacked hard into the reef.

Startled, delirious, the two unharmed little birds shook off, looked curiously at the mussels and Turkish towel seaweed. Not their usual haunt. And then they flew away. I paddled near where they'd fallen, saw a purple crab half ingested by a green anemone. One pincer still reached out of the quicksand mouth, opening and closing reflexively. A gull waddled about in the shallows with a sixteen-legged purple sunflower star in its mouth—an obscene mass of little tentacle-lined legs dangling from the gull's slender beak. Those tiny transparent tentacles were tube feet, with which to suck and pull, squirt out sticky mucous when the star had scrambled after chitons and sea cucumbers. Urchins, seemingly stationary little prickler balls, are said to flee an approaching sunflower star, to crawl over one another and occasionally get spit off by a fellow urchin and into the gaping mouth of a hungry anemone. But when a star catches up to an urchin, it devours the urchin whole and discards only the scoured tines. When I went back among the waves, a soft light shot a skin over the water's depth. Countless distinct little swells: from the wake of the board, paddling hands, micro rills running up minirogue convergences of backwash and evening wind swell. When watched long enough, *almost* decipherable.

The otter drifted nearby in the multiplying kelp, getting fat on the fecund spring upwelling; northwesterlies churned up the water and brought masses of nutrients from the deep. And him, too: today, there was another otter, a playmate, lighter of color and smaller. They thrashed and rolled among thick strands of feather boa, lost urchins and mussels so painfully harvested. Until today I'd assumed this guy avoided women, thought the hassle of the whole affair turned him off—courtship lasting days, male expected to inquisitively bump the female for half an hour (if she snubs him, he'll often steal an urchin in outrage). But today, she was harassing back, and no jealous pup interfering. So I watched for her to go rigid, belly up. He'd swim beneath, reach around and claw her breasts, stretch his head around and bite onto her nose, then do some complicated contortions to get it in there. Could last up to fourteen minutes. How I'd love to have witnessed the rumored pillow talk afterwards, the mutual grooming and napping and the occasional second round. They never did get to any down-to-business thrashing, and I supposed it was just as well since that nose bite can be lethal. A local biologist once watched a male kill two females during mating and tow the second around for a day, trying to force-feed her corpse. In the official report: "definitely aberrant behavior." (Compared to what?)

I started back to shore, sex not being much of a spectator sport, but before I could let the whole scene go, a lone gull flew from the cliff straight out to sea. It flew with purpose, I imagined, after whatever school of baitfish the flock outside was feeding on. And just when it struck me that I alone in this crowd wasn't working, the gull suddenly doubled back, soared into an incoming wave, and brought the whole issue to a head. It banked hard at water level, pulled into the cushion of air preceding the swell, and glided along the face. It kept a high line with perfect trim, riding a wind wave made by a water wave made by wind. I turned and watched the gull pass; the wave rolled under me and I watched its back, desperate to know how far the gull would go. Not until the wave collapsed on the sand did the gull pop into the air above and U-turn toward the flock: no clear purpose, no desired gain of distance. Quite literally, just surfing. Too familiar . . . late morning, existential questions creeping once again: what was, after all, the point? "*n*. 2. a projecting part of anything: *A point of land juts into the bay*"? Yes, of course that, but—"3. something having a sharp or tapering end"? Not so much when looking along the cove, but perhaps—"9. a degree or stage: *frankness to the point of insult*"? No, no, how about, "10. a particular instant of time"? Yes, of course! A year, a day, a life! And even, "12. the important or essential thing: *the point of the matter*."

23

Killing a slow, waveless afternoon at Willie's place after a fruitless fifty-mile search. This week the farmers had plowed under the coast, and the brussels sprout "speedlings" were on their way in; crops grow while the wild strips sleep. Watched the taut, snapping hover of a flock of Bonaparte's gulls plucking worms from a drying field under a fierce northwesterly, wind giving their flight an agitation utterly consistent with the season's business. Such stylized colors on those small gulls: sharp black masks on their faces, bodies like little gift-shop carvings. And such peace in watching the wind's vicissitudes from afar, still more dust rising from that tractor and a cormorant gunning south on an express current. Willie played his custom rosewood guitar for several hours while I took in the view, the instrument's small, tapered sound box ringing bright while two crows looped about in their nutty mixture of gaiety and malevolence, coyotes of the air. And over the fields, past cattle grazing on the promontory outside Willie's home, the Santa Lucias loomed over Point Lobos. I needed to know—and didn't, quite—why the dark harrier banking the field before us stirred me the way it did, its patterns such a palimpsest of energy and murder and the rhythms and circles of air. There is a way in which the stiff tilting of spread wings and the bird's brushing of willow thickets seem a traceless painting of this small world's shapes. And finally the hawk becomes the very symbol for me of the spirit of this coast: in a static hover against the north wind, wings in a high V, beak hooked under and eyes riveted on the green grass. All on a hill high above the sea cliff, frozen before a red sun setting as a fat, burning ball over the water. If there's a relief in discovering the life you most desperately dream of living, there's also a fear in discovering your soul's needs—after all, how then deny them?

The fog bank far off Willie's porch swirled again in a building cloud of abstracted ocean, roiling and waving in the slow silence with which air carries on. It grew and billowed over the cliffs far below the hillside and I saw still more of the life of fog, more small things I would never have noticed had I not been on this coast all year (a blink in time, really, compared to that spent by Vince or Willie), like a prow of gray droplets reaching across a lagoon like the bow of a ghost schooner, the free agency of a disconnected cloud. It's unsettling to discover how hard-won is real understanding of place, how much it demands stillness and time; *real* time, daily visitation, walks to the Point or drives clear to the edge of the county when not the faintest swell is showing. Unsettling like a first glimpse, in the company of a new companion, of how much one might actually love that other: so much more seems suddenly possible, and yet no way to rush it. As I sat there listening to Willie's fingerpicking—he was a brilliant guitarist—the aimless eye caught a female marsh hawk, large and pale, lifting herself out of a field of radish blossoms and beating across a ravine of dry grass. Then the male flapped up from the same field and followed; they flew together awhile, carving small arcs until she settled back into the flowers. He paused nearby on an old fence post by an oak tree. Ten minutes passed with the male immobile before he spread his wings and drifted off his perch, floated over to her spot in the grass and fell down with her, out of my view. She wasn't ready yet, and before he'd folded his wings she flapped into the air and beat her way over to the fence post. They played this languid, patient game of hard-to-get for nearly an hour: even the killers, in love! An anthropomorphization, of course—a sentimentality—but assuming their musical nests to be mating byplay, why not assume behaviorist language captures as little of hawk love as it would of ours?

Reverie broken by the setting sun, I drove home to a funny contrast: the Germans, back in my kitchen after less than a week, sheepish and not quite happy to see me.

"Costa Rica," Thore said when I asked, "not so good."

No? I looked to Mitch.

He put his face on the table. "Nooo," he said, shaking his head. He sat up and looked out the window at our little street, a picture of the ordinary. He chuckled nervously. "Not so good."

"Beaches dirty," Thore added, "no waves. Very dirty. Ve come home."

All the way? A letter-a-day had arrived for Thore, perfumed and addressed in a flowery hand. The four latest seemed to take even more wind out of his exploring sails.

"No," Thore said, "we buy a van maybe now. See California. Maybe one month." He looked a little sick. The Wild West . . . he hadn't caught more than ten waves. Mitch looked blank, disconsolate—love, the old traitor, had done him in. They settled for a blue-and-gray '67, bought from a UC Santa Cruz student for thirteen hundred dollars, and asked where to go.

Hey, well, Yosemite? Mendocino? San Francisco? Joshua Tree? Disneyland? Rincon? Hard to go wrong!

One morning a few days later, on my prebreakfast surf check, I found them parked by the cliff again. They'd never left the city limits, but they had plastered the van with stickers: Irie Vibrations, Byrning Spears, No Fear, Pearson Arrow Surfboards. Mitch sat sullenly in the sliding door, his bare feet on the pavement. Thore, leaning against the cliff railing, ate a bowl of cereal. "I think I go," he said, milk dribbling into his new goatee.

Germany?

"Yah."

I looked at Mitch, who chuckled again and scrutinized his hands: three weeks, two thousand dollars, and he hadn't wanted to surf that bad to begin with.

"And you?" I asked.

"Oh," he said, searching, "I stay. Tourism."

Thore flew out the next morning, broke. "I think I go travel in Europe," he said as he got in the shuttle. Quite sick of the coast, Mitch asked again for directions to Yosemite; I told him about a hot spring and a few good hikes, said he'd need warmer clothes, insisted he stay with us when he returned. After all, he'd been the second child of the pair, less winning but also less comfortable being the hapless youth. Like myself, he lacked the emotional fortitude of the solitary wanderer.

The next morning he was parked on the cliff again—Yosemite?

"No . . . but this morning," he said, looking interested in something for the first time, "and five mornings. Six o'clock, guy on a bicycle comes and"—he made a sound as of drawing mucous from the back of his throat—"then, phhhttt! Right . . . here!" He pointed at the windshield, livid. "So, last night, I not sleep." He was a big guy, with thick, hard arms, and the army had probably taught him something about hurting people. "I wait all night," he said, smacking fist into palm and squinting murderously.

I looked around for signs of a struggle—a bike wrapped around a pole maybe, or a little blood on the pavement. "You kill him?" I asked.

"I fall asleep for *one minute*!" he said, burning with rage. "And

I wake up to hear *smack* on the window! I jump out and . . . he is gone! AAARRGGHHH!" All the frustrations of this pathetic trip focused on ripping the head off some vicious kid, and again he'd failed. "Must to sell the van," he said.

So we put an ad in the paper and he started parking in different places, looking out to sea all day, occasionally trying to read a local free paper. The only call was from the guy who'd sold the bus to them in the first place, offering five hundred dollars to take it back. Mitch couldn't stand the indignity, so he entrusted the sale to my housemate Keith in exchange for a twenty percent surcharge; I offered $150 for Mitch's surfboard, a beautiful twin-zer worth a lot more, but he wanted *something* to show for his travels, so he decided to keep it. The morning he left, Mitch mentioned getting a job at home, staying put, taking up cycling.

A few weeks later, Keith came into the kitchen.

"Look," he said, "this guy's interested in the bus, but I'm thinking maybe if I hold on to it, do like a bunch of repairs, you know, really fix her up . . ."

Yeah?

"Well, it'd be great to have it through the summer, you know? So like in the fall I could sell it for more and we'd *both* get more money and I'd get wheels, and anyway, I want to learn how to surf, and I could put my board in back and maybe take it down to Baja?"

Mitch, ten thousand miles away, watching the mail, waiting for a check.

24

Night falls differently over the open coast than in town: no streetlights adding sparkle, no electric constellation replacing the fading liquid one. The watery world and sky out there dusking into darkness along field, pond, beach, and ravine—such a unified experience for an otherwise variegated terrain. There's something powerfully calming about a summer sunset on such a south-facing seacoast. The sun falls behind land, out of sight to the right and casting a soft glow evenly across everything. No offshore fireworks as in winter, and none of the certain closure of a sun inching across the horizon's absolute date line—just a gentle slip from evening light into night itself. On Willie's deck again, I watched a farm truck inch through the sprouts far below, a fishing boat's little lights come on. Tried to look forward to a summer divided between Berkeley and the Sierra, to leaving town until fall; Willie and Pascale were off to Indonesia through October; Vince and Fran back to Europe. A tabby cat prowled the dried, seeding mustard beyond the garden as Pascale crumpled up newspaper to light the grill. After reading how a local Pinot Noir had beaten all the world-class French Pinots, Willie had driven up to the Santa Cruz Mountains and bought a case: wood, smoke, and fruit, an orchestrated cloud of flavor dissipating as a whole, no one taste lingering out of context. We watched whales spout and breach out there, heading north—every few minutes a tiny plume of white. Scraping off the grill, Pascale told Fran about her poetry, how it was mostly confessional and how she couldn't imagine working in prose. All the stage props between epiphanies would just kill her. Fran, who only knew Pascale casually, asked a question I didn't catch, and Pascale answered that she just liked the meticulous crafting of a moment, small music over and over again. Nothing self-dramatizing about the way she said this, just something she clearly loved doing.

Willie, looking very much the elegant host, brought a platter of seafood and a bowl of marinade from the kitchen. He and Pascale had their barbecue scene wired, so Vince and I sat on a bench facing west. No car sounds, no city sounds, not even the roar of the sea. The university term was about over and Vince had only a stack of final exams between him and three months of marginal summer surf. He was quite happy longboarding tiny waves on hot days, not to mention riding whatever south swell we got from Baja hurricanes; his nine-foot nose rider had so much glide that even a knee-high rill could make him happy. He talked about his work as though it were merely a clever means of sustaining all that surfing, but I was certain he was a brilliant teacher. He had the kind of loose, direct charm that makes you enjoy what you're learning, look forward to the classroom. Pascale, apparently a line chef in a prior life, lay the prawns near the edges of the grill, the two lobsters in the middle, and oysters throughout. While she splashed on a little wine, I asked how she and Willie had landed this beautiful place. For one thing, I knew you couldn't just rent apartments on the coast: it was all zoned agricultural, with these buildings intended strictly to house farm employees. It turned out that when Willie moved back to California, after several years between Bali and a string of islands off Sumatra, he'd wanted to replicate the lives led over there, the third-world space and time zone. Knocked at every worker encampment north of town looking for a room, but no luck. People thought he was nuts. And then, right after he married Pascale, the basil guy she worked for offered them *this* beautiful place—arrival. Good things come in twos.

Increasingly drunk, I got called upon to make the paella rice. So, back indoors to sauté it first in olive oil, then boil it in chicken stock with red and yellow peppers, heaps of garlic and saffron. They had big iron pots, beautiful chopping blocks, and well-sharpened knives, but much of the apartment was loose ends: musical scores lay about and one wall had been left unplastered. While chopping a white onion, Fran mentioned her doctoral thesis on bodies, pleasure, and power in the San Francisco gay bathhouses. It occurred to me that Michel Foucault, the late French philosopher who'd come out of the closet in those baths, shared much with Richard Henry Dana, Jack London, and thousands of surfers having found themselves in California's waters, but Fran wasn't impressed, sensed something untoward in the suggestion; perhaps she was right. Conversation moved to the question of which cutting board they'd designated for garlic—wouldn't want to ruin the next morning's sliced melon—and soon we all seated ourselves around a handmade cedar table before a wall of windows. I lucked out and got the chair facing off the edge of North America, and Pascale served organic artichokes from the basil man's private fields: big buds on white plates with homemade herbed mayonnaise. The sea outside was now dark save for a region of red along the distant part of the earth's curve, a little glimpse of yesterday leaking over backwards. Willie directed our attention to the sunset's sublimity, and conversation turned to moments-of-beauty-one-has-never-forgotten. Willie described surfing alone at dawn and watching three killer whales surface around him, their curved black fins glistening in the daybreak. Vince, with ironic composure, told of a time in his wilder days when a local shaper had left a bag of peyote buttons and a stilettolike board on his porch. He'd gobbled up in the woods with a friend, hung out for a while with two white dogs, then ended up down at Steamer Lane on an offshore fall afternoon with sharp-edged six-foot peaks rolling through. Whatever the 1970s had been around here, everyone at the table remembered them as strikingly different from the present. Vince gave an animated description of riding that little blade through a big, falling tube, how he saw, through its opening, the trailing rainbow of the prior wave and four gulls flying along the lip, the whole thing a life-changing time warp until the barrel shut down and clobbered him.

Vince and Willie and I indulged in surfing talk for a while, and then Pascale cleared her throat. "Skiing recently," she said, nodding, "above Lake Tahoe. I wasn't on the hard runs or anything, but all the snow kept everyone else from driving up, so we got the whole mountain to ourselves, floating through—okay, I'll use the word—*virgin* powder." She laughed, then continued: "And the crazy thing was, I never really felt the bottom with my skis. It was kind of like floating on a goose-down cushion, but made of dry ice. All those little crystals flew behind us in drifting angel trails." We all paused a moment, pictured it. Willie and Vince looked at each other: angel trails . . . metaphor or assertion?

"These artichokes," said Fran, "are just . . . shall we say, very special?" She closed her eyes and pulled a leaf slowly between teeth and tongue. And then, treat of sensual treats: asparagus. That, too, was served nearly plain, their confidence in the produce great enough to feel that "the thing itself" would only suffer in the company of distracting textures and tastes. With Vince's nudging,

Fran offered an uncharacteristic and surprising epiphany of her own, one from a prior marriage: descending from high camp above the clouds on a Central American volcano, a hundred-mile view over unearthly cirrus fleece, dropping through the cloud layer to mountainsides of bright red and yellow opium poppies. She shivered at the memory as though it confirmed the supremacy of intuition over linearity. Vince fished for more details, apparently not having heard the story before, but Fran insisted that was the only relevant part, that she'd give him the rest later. And then mine: a long, slow morning on a ledge high on El Capitan, our fifth day of the climb, my stoned climbing partners fumbling around while I floated six hours away with my sock feet hanging off a 2,800-foot drop, deep into juice-fast spaciness and yang utterly purged, watching a peregrine falcon ride high updrafts for miles across its vast hunting ground, never once flapping. But my story, like the others, sat flat on the table over the huge paella pan, a clutching at the grail offered as evidence of its presence, a question offered as proof of its hoped-for answer.

Digging into a plate of prawns, Vince mentioned a great novel he'd read recently, how it extended the whole westering archetype to the surfer who vanishes into the South Pacific. As he outlined the plot, I took a few bites and settled comfortably into the mood of our shared sacrifices and devotions. "One thing seems weird about it," he said into his food, forking an oyster from its shell, "is that to anybody who's inside surfing, you know it doesn't mean shit."

I looked up. Willie looked up.

"Well," Vince insisted, his jaw set, "it doesn't." All those years given to such a beautiful pursuit, and still so much doubt. I didn't agree, didn't even believe he meant it, but perhaps only because the price had, as yet, been so much lower for me.

25

Fog wind and flat light on the last day I surfed the Point before leaving town: even in the late afternoon, big wisps of mist whipped past turned-over fields (the yellow all yanked), and wild plants between them showing the recent late rain—bloomed hemlock still billowing. Radish and mustard blossoms drying, an effusion of sage green: a less neon contrast already, a more tasteful, desert-plants canvas. The whole coast west of the highway not yet planted, soil dried a bit, a flock of seagulls following a tractor, eating the upturned worms. Agriculture happening—the empty seed rows littered with sprouts. Hills overgrown, unkempt and drying, foxtails waving in the parching wind and poppies riding high among the drying pastures: the leaves of grass were fresh at their roots, but pale above, so the poppies appeared as floating planes of pointillism, carpets of vibrant orange hovering over beds of green. Gulls feasted on a passing school of fish, and hundreds of frogs croaked in the rail-ditch lily pond; for once, the chickadees, red-winged blackbirds, swallows, and sparrows all outsang the distant white noise of the small surf.

Four brown pelicans in their spring molt—gray with white underfeathers, brown necks and white heads—stood on the black sea stack where the hill's grassy slope ended at a rocky tidal flat; one life stopping, the other starting, all within ten feet. Something about their resting posture, their heads pulled back and bills flat against their necks, struck me as preternaturally appalled. Then one stretched out its broad wings, rearranging feathers, and another reached its long, long bill up in the air like a dinosaur trumpeter swan, loosening the dried pink flesh of its gular sac. Their skeletons seemed oddly complex and mechanical, and they just stood together, a little delegation, not talking or squawking. Then they flapped into formation, rounded the rock, and caught a south breeze in single file, with stately, steady wingbeats on the bow wave of turbulence just off a swell, like porpoises surfing the wake of a tanker, though without their playfulness of purpose. With synchronized flapping pushing the same air, they drafted like bicyclists, each bird producing an updraft on which its follower floated. The lead pelican eventually peeled off, drifted to the back, and let another do the work. Far outside, they rose over a floating flock of gulls, and began to circle: anchovies, sardines, perhaps mackerel. Then the leader pulled in its wings, drew back its head, and plummeted. Down, at a hard angle into the water, air sacs in its breast breaking the impact—fish as deep as two meters stunned by the shock. (As a pelican's bill enters, the upper mandible snaps down on the widely bowed lower one, slamming the fish into the open pouch.) It surfaced quickly, pouch sagging under two gallons of water. A minute later, when its pouch had drained, the pelican lifted up its bill and choked down whatever it had caught. Far offshore, in the fog, passed an enormous Hyundai container ship.

Stepping to the beach, I went, in two steps, from twelve orange poppies in a patch to rounded surf cobble colonized by furtive crabs. The moon had been pulling very low tides, but morning fog shielded the exposed invertebrates from the sun. Whole tidal worlds lay revealed, naked and wet like a raw skin under the gray ceiling of mist. A flock of seagulls stood around the shallows plucking up starfish, tearing at sea grapes, shitting their smothering guano on the struggling sea moss. And, with all this bare, bands of life stood clear: the drab barnacles, snails, and nailbrush of the highest, driest rocks; then, a bit lower, the rockweeds and a few dangling seaweeds, and then leather chitons mowing mottled coralline crusts, and, below it all, a curtain of blooming surf grass covering light-bulb tunicates. Borderlands of varying degree, a world of margins and flux. All those barnacles throwing open their doors and reaching out after food when water flooded over, a few probing around with their filament penises.

Tiny waves . . . I poked around for a while in the shallows, resisting the inevitable. Waited as the fog pulled out, slept for a while on the beach. Made lousy use of my time by sticking a hardened stick of seaweed into an anemone, watching it squirt and contract. Backed a little rock crab into a corner and dueled with his monstrous Popeye arms, fed a starfish to an anemone, but pulled it right back out. Rows of sea palms gave and swayed as I waded through the shallows with my board—air and water both in the fifties. I supposed there was a recycling, an eco*system*, in all these savage little worlds, but derive a life? A code? From Ed Ricketts's 1939 *Between Pacific Tides*: "Our visitor to a rocky shore at low tide has entered possibly the most prolific life zone in the world—a belt so thickly populated that often not only is every square inch of the area utilized by some plant or animal but the competition for attachment sites is so keen that animals settle upon each other—plants grow upon animals, and animals upon plants." Or, in *Cannery Row*, in which Ricketts figures as a character and John Steinbeck intentionally socks it to Ricketts with a moral about those who would romanticize the wild: "Here a crab tears a leg from his brother . . . Then the creeping murderer, the octopus, steals out, slowly, softly, moving like a gray mist, pretending to be a bit of weed, now a rock, now a lump of decaying meat while its evil goat eyes watch coldly." It's Melville's universal cannibalism of the sea, where Ricketts sees in the horror of the glassed-over pool a "lovely, colored world"—tide pool as evasive simulacrum.

Walking over those mossy boulders and reefs, slipping and falling toward the deeper water, blood and snot mingling on a wetsuit soaked with sweat and urine—up to the knees in that glass, toes squishing on the reef's fleshy pavement, wondering. In "The Love Song of J. Alfred Prufrock," when T. S. Eliot grows weary of the burden of consciousness, he writes that he "should have been a pair of ragged claws / Scuttling across the floors of silent seas." Rock crab? Shrimp? Or just a figure of speech? Hands numb, ice-cream headaches from ducking frigid waves. Pawing and pulling the surfboard across great tangles and shafts of bull kelp that floated like shiny vines and tree limbs. A forest reaching through the murk like long, waving ivy without a house to hang on—twisted braids of life. The matted canopy absorbed wave shock, kept the surf calm in high seas, waved in liquid columns like spineless trees dangling from the sky, inhaling up with the surf curve's sine, exhaling down with its cosine. The breathing pulse of life as insensate momentum. Down there in the light-dappled jungle, bat stars and black abalone crowded the rubbery holdfasts; crabs and snails nibbled the stipes and got nibbled by rockfish, kelp bass, and surfperch: the obscenely numerous little scavengings and assaults of an exquisite organization.

Tried to take off on a little wave, but fell over on the drop—legs stiff, no balance. But at least I was wet. Paddled for another, but didn't judge it right. A boil formed below and the lip threw me headfirst. The fog finally drew out as evening came, and another man stood on the cliffs. A seal surfaced nearby, and then vanished. The sun threw long shadows across the cliffs, etched out little caves and hollows. The water was a hard blue-black, with a rose dusk spangled across its ripples. Caught a few more waves, but couldn't warm up. The seal appeared again, fishing among the exposed reefs. Much later, in the last half hour of light, the other guy paddled out. It was Steve, the one with the little blind dog. We chatted a bit, and got cold together in the same frigid water as the sun lowered, lighting cliff arretes and darkening long sediment fractures. A regal pelican floated neck upright, beak straight down. The cold breeze and lack of waves meant no adrenaline at all and I started shivering. The sharp sun was a very clear ball. Steve said he was moving back to Utica, New York, to live with his brother and take nursing prerequisites at a community college. After ten years, California just hadn't worked out: wife finally gone, economy awful, cities so big and expensive. He started shivering too, though he'd only been out a little while. I could see his jaw clenched, his shoulders hunched tight. Wasn't looking forward to Eastern winters, he said, once thought he'd seen his last.

The sun fattened out along the bottom and melted quickly into the ocean as he talked—beautiful, but so chilling. I paddled in alone, shook all over in violent, jerking spasms as I pulled off my wetsuit. Took awhile to get dressed; my fingers were so numb I had to button my jeans by opposition between my palms. And all that time, Steve stayed in the water, not even trying for waves, just drifting about with his hands before him in the growing night. Even when I'd changed and the sun had set completely, he remained. Walking back across the fields, I could still see wisps of cloud in the darkness; headlights appeared on the highway while back there at the cliff's edge, the cypresses flattened into silhouettes against the remaining strip of purple dusk. Silence, breathing . . . footsteps away from that black sea, more a frigid embalming fluid than Lethean warmth. No doctor would ever send a patient here to recover lost youth. Held underwater by a cold, dark wave, one feels too much infirmity, one's body being, after all, so aqueous.

Epilogue

There's a last encounter I want to include in this book; it's not about surfing, but it is about whatever drove me to seek the kind of peace surfing offers. I had my truck packed and Susan was expecting me for lunch in Berkeley the next day, so I walked down to the cliff railing for the last in what had been a year of great sunsets. First, I saw the architect again, leaning against the rail: he too had the spring northwesterlies on his mind. Trying to write a poem about the cypress outside his window, how it revealed to him the wind's every move, the swirling world pinned down by his beach-shack panopticon.

I wondered aloud if he knew a poem by A. R. Ammons: "The reeds give / way to the / wind and give / the wind away."

No, he admitted, but Jeffers on whitecapping: the sea as "whitened with the falcon's passage." Not mythological, he insisted, citing the chaos-theory example of the butterfly's wings in Arabia causing a hurricane in Florida. And poetry, he said, was like that butterfly, the .02 percent along the bottom of the bell curve that we always cut off, imagining it to be insignificant. Thus the appeal of the sea, a commitment to the mundane unknowable, a daily dose of the wild. "Step off that beach," he said, "you're in true wilderness. No either/or, no halfway. Those energies right there" —and he pointed to a big, breeze-sculpted wave line—"a geometry in chaos, unhindered by man. Nothing slows or changes that energy. It just is. And you feel it even walking on the beach and meeting eyes with a sea lion."

(Ammons again: "I found a / weed / that had a / mirror in it / and that / mirror / looked in at / a mirror / in / me that / had a / weed in it.") I told him about that awful day alone, in monstrous, foaming, frothing walls, about being quite scared.

He bristled a little, said he preferred swimming naked.

"I gave up that whole equipment thing long ago," he said. "I just like to, you know," and he made a motion with his broad, sun-flecked hand of slipping and pulsing through water. "Sure, there's stuff in it that shouldn't be there, and the crap that's just in the water and the air, that's everywhere. But I'm not so concerned with the ecology. I'm more into the energy itself, just that liquid force on my body."

But, I told him, those big, ten-foot churning beasts . . . boy, that's a lot of energy, you know?

"USS *Wasp*," he said with a shrug, eyes on the ground, "aircraft carrier off the Philippines, we were charging eighty-foot glassy mountains of water. As the boat dipped down to one side, you'd see water as high as that cypress over there, the big green one on top of the hill." I looked over, distracted for a moment from the size of my own waves, and saw the great tree silhouetted black against the late afternoon sun above a concrete statue of a whale. "Then the ship would turn and you'd see nothing but sky; then down again. And then I heard the faintest sound of an old diesel engine—'put, put, put'—a small, Chinese fishing boat, just three guys calmly puttering up one mountain and down the other. That night, while I was trying to sleep, the bow kept punching into the bases of these waves, and the whole thousand-foot aircraft carrier would shake, and knock my skull against the bulkhead."

"Well, my uncle," I said, by way of reflexive competition, "he's a captain for Chevron on the Anchorage to San Diego oil run. Says he's hit bigger surf than that coming out of the shit-chute in the Gulf of Alaska, waves wrapping around the tanker and ripping off cranes and catwalks."

The architect let that soak in, squinted at a squat, rectangular fishing vessel by the pier. "Wilderness all right," he said. "That's why I live here. You've got to go a helluva long ways north to find another." We both watched a little boy waddle down to the beach with a bucket and shovel; changing the subject, I told him I'd been poking around in a few tide pools.

"I'm not much of a tide-pooler," he said quickly, looking away, "they're too intimate. You really invade them when you walk around and collect stuff. No," he said, squinting away again, "I don't need to gather . . . or name."

Enough said, we stood quietly for a moment, each nodded slightly, and then he raised his eyebrows in closure and walked off for his solo beach stroll; breeze and water lapped at the sand, wood smoke in the air from the season's first few beach fires. The little stucco studios were cluttered with flower boxes and tricycles, and a row of new little palms stood outside the woman painter's door. In an old brown Chrysler two young men in black sunglasses drank beers without talking; two surfboards lay in the backseat. I leaned against the rail and, as I imagined they were doing as well, visualized big lines rolling in off the horizon, an unseasonable swell—like imagining snow in the tropics. A man on the beach below in a black gee and red belt spread out a blanket and lay a martial arts sword and staff parallel on one side. Another six-inch rill washed over the sand, then drained. The driver of the sedan looked into his beer. I bent over to stretch and saw the ninja below face inland with feet apart and fists clenched, breathing deeply as if gathering courage. Suddenly, he sprang into the air, spun to face the ocean, and high-kicked with both feet. When he landed, he thrust hard with each fist, then stopped cold. A woman walked her Doberman along the sand before him.

The usual earnest conversations meandered along the surf, and in a burgundy Chevrolet pickup, through the lens of a dashboard-mounted telescope, a fat man with a flaccid face and empty eyes scrutinized a couple lying by the water. Then his wife walked up barefoot, very tan with beautiful silver hair and a grim composure to her step. She reached into the truck and grabbed a pair of binoculars; he said nothing to her, didn't look away from the telescope. She walked alone to the wooden sunset bench and folded her legs beneath her on the seat, and then she too was watching people; though while her gaze moved around quickly, impatiently, his remained on the couple—seeing them, perhaps, as well as they saw each other. When I turned away and walked back past a yellow, paint-chipping bungalow with its potted plants and little wind-powered wooden seagull, the driver of the Chrysler smacked his palm on the dashboard and damned the placid Pacific. Steel-blue sunset now, with a wash of purple tint; two freighters loomed black against a red band of sky, and clouds halfway over the horizon stood like mysterious, intemporal islands, mountains, spires.

The painter's studio door creaked open and there she stood by a disemboweled file cabinet on her cement stoop. We'd spoken a few times in the last month, and I'd grown to like her very much.

I asked how she was, and she rubbed a palm on her paint-splattered jeans, tried to decide which version to give. "Oh," she said, with a glance to the sky, "I'm having a little operation tomorrow. Not a big one, just . . . I'm fine." She smiled absurdly behind her sunglasses. Slipped her long feet into pink slippers before stepping onto the sidewalk.

"So," I said, trying not to imply a need for sympathy, "nothing life-threatening?"

"Well, it's a cancer biopsy."

Hmm: the light had drained off the land and out to sea, leaving the water wildly luminescent against the dark earth.

"So, you know," she said, "what would *you* do if it were the last night of your life?"

I glanced at her hands, took a simpatico guess: "Scotch and a cigarette on the cliff?"

"Yeah, that." She nodded, looking at the full tumbler in one hand, flicking an ash with the other. "I painted till six," she said with false cheer, exhaustion audible in her pauses between syllables, "which is late for me. Maybe bake bread."

"Least it'll knead back," I offered. "You can check the stars between risings."

"That's why I live here."

"Daily contact with the inhuman vast?"

She thought about this, sighed as she looked down the block; the ocean had now faded to a black far deeper than that ashore. She shook her head: "Nah."